TEACHERS WHO LEAD

The Rhetoric of Reform
and
the Realities of Practice

Patricia A. Wasley, 1951-

TEACHERS
COLLEGE
PRESS

Teachers College, Columbia University
New York and London

Published by Teachers College Press, 1234 Amsterdam Avenue
New York, NY 10027

Library of Congress Cataloging-in-Publication Data

Wasley, Patricia A., 1951–
    Teachers who lead : the rhetoric of reform and the realities of
practice / Patricia A. Wasley.
        p.   cm.   —   (Professional development and practice series)
    Includes bibliographical references (p.   ) and index.
    ISBN 0-8077-3104-8 (alk. paper).—ISBN 0-8077-3103-X (pbk.: alk. paper)
    1. Master teachers—United States—Case studies.   2. Teaching.
I. Title.   II. Series.
LB2832.2.W38   1991
371.1'02—dc20   91-15600

ISBN 0-8077-3104-8
ISBN 0-8077-3103-X (pbk.)

Printed on acid-free paper
Manufactured in the United States of America

97 96 95 94 93 92 91   8 7 6 5 4 3 2 1

To Gwen, Ted, and Mary
for sharing both problems and paradoxes.

To Kate Wasley, Ruth Emery, and Ann Lieberman
for teaching me about possibilities.

Contents

Foreword

This volume is a wonderfully fresh addition to the Professional Development and Practice Series. Patricia Wasley tells the stories of three teacher leaders, setting them within the context of the reform movement as well as their own lives. She brings a remarkable, unaffected authenticity to her work that the reader will enjoy. The work of these three teachers as they struggle in their own ways to change the practice of teaching involves us in the contemporary effort to expand the concept of teaching to include leaders who both teach students and significantly influence their colleagues.

But how does this come about in a bureaucratic system where all roles are already structured? What tensions do teachers experience as they try to step out of the traditional structure and rethink their use of time, place, and curricula, redefining teaching in the process? How do these pathfinders actually work? What assumptions do they make about their work? And what do their peers think of them?

All of these questions and more are the grist for this very original book about three teachers in leadership positions. We come to know them as people in their own classrooms and schools, hard-working men and women unafraid to tackle the system that has restricted their work. And, through Wasley's deep knowledge and affection, we come to better understand the dilemmas and demands they face as well as the power and passion they demonstrate in filling these roles. Each of them has a unique view of the teacher's place in the system as well as of teaching itself. Each is strongly committed to teaching, teachers, and students. Each goes about his or her work in a different way. All however, work long days, are deeply committed to changing existing practice, and are immersed in "teaching" and "leading". Their stories can't help but engage any reader who cares deeply about the teaching profession.

Wasley, as a former teacher leader, feels the joy and the pain of being a pathfinder, and so do we, her audience. This volume will enhance our understanding of what teacher leadership is, what it is attempting to accomplish, and what it can be. Without romanticizing the view that teachers can expand their role and serve as leaders for one another, Wasley has written a book of struggle, passion, and commitment. It will take its place as the primer on teacher leadership and thus help set the terms for the ongoing debate about this important part of the endeavor to reform the nation's schools.

Ann Lieberman, Editor.

Acknowledgments

This book is truly the product of a number of collaborative relationships between my colleagues in schools and my colleagues in universities. The cases are the result of time spent in three important classrooms with a number of teachers, principals, and students who shared their frustrations and their dreams, and thought with me about unfamiliar things. They then read what I had written, wrote notes, and worked with me until we came to shared understandings about teacher leadership as it appeared in their particular context. Although we agreed to respect their anonymity, clearly this book would not exist without their willingness to participate and to share openly. On a more personal note, I have been enormously enriched by my association with Ted and Gwen and Mary.

The research was originally reported in my doctoral dissertation completed in 1989 at the University of Washington entitled "The Rhetoric of Reform and the Realities of Practice: A Study of Teacher Leaders." (The methodology used to conduct these cases is more thoroughly explained in the Appendix.) The original work was supported by the Puget Sound Educational Consortium, a partnership between the University of Washington and 14 school districts in the Seattle area. This collaboration, designed to create better schools, provided financial support as well as the opportunity to work with more than 100 teachers who held leadership positions in their districts.

The rewriting has been supported by the Coalition of Essential Schools, a partnership between Brown University and participating schools and states across the country. This collaboration has provided me with a forum of teachers, principals, and policymakers with whom to discuss the ideas contained in this volume.

The book has been enormously strengthened by a number of people who read successive drafts, offered clear-sighted suggestions, and then urged me on. They are Ken Sirotnik, Walter Parker, and Edgar Winans at the University of Washington; Joe McDonald and Paula Evans at Brown University; and Lynne Miller at the University of Southern Maine. Brian Ellerbeck, from Teachers College Press, edited with great care. His suggestions increased the depth of the book. Lillian Ruemeli, Susan Fisher, Alixe Callen, and Rachel Sherman figured out all the technological details as we swapped disks, and then they read and reread as we prepared the final manuscript. Rick Lear, also from Brown, patiently read draft after draft, pushing me toward greater clarity.

I gained inspiration and clearer understanding from conversations with John Goodlad. Ted Sizer provided great encouragement, a sense of the validity of the ideas, and then put a "gone fishing" sign on my office so that I could write. Finally, I had unabashed support, prompting, and cheering from Ann Lieberman, without whom I would never have attempted such a project.

TEACHERS WHO LEAD

The Rhetoric of Reform
and
the Realities of Practice

CHAPTER 1

Teacher Leadership: Current Rhetoric or Everyday Reality?

In 1976, my second year of teaching, I was asked to take on a new responsibility—a teacher leadership position. My job was to help set up an advisory program in a large urban high school of about 2,000 students. I was one of four teachers selected for this position, and the only woman. The hope was that we would design something that would enable each teacher in the school to get to know 25 students very well and to see them through their 4 years in the school, to monitor their personal as well as their educational welfare, so that teachers might feel better able to contribute to student success. For the students, the hope was that the large, impersonal high school would become more familiar and accessible, and that students would develop a stronger support system within the school to help them to cope with the trials and tribulations inherent in the lives of adolescents. I was paid an additional $3,000 per year—about a fifth of my salary—and was given one extra planning period per day in order to help design and implement the program.

I was surprised but thrilled at the offer made by the principal, readily accepted the job, and raced off to tell my friends. My closest friend, an art teacher who had been teaching 10 years in the school, burst into tears when I gave her the news. These were not tears of joy; she was totally unable to celebrate with me, as she very much wanted the position herself. I felt wounded by her response and confused but never considered giving the position up. I had, after all, been chosen by the administration, and I, too, wanted the job.

During the ensuing year, there was considerable grumbling among the faculty about the positions, about who'd been selected, and about the concept of advisory. Some people were angry because a young woman had been selected. Many women were angry because three men had been selected. Almost everyone was mad about being required to take on additional responsibility and made comments like, "Pretty soon we'll be doing the kids' homework with them, too," and "Drug and alcohol counseling, expanded curriculum, new standardized tests at every level, and now family groups?" There was no forum for public discussion that allowed people to vent their discontent or to investigate the rationale for the roles, so most of the kvetching was done around the lunch tables or in the faculty room out of earshot of the administrators.

The four of us who held the leadership positions felt fortunate to have a new opportunity. We felt privileged. We tended to avoid the most obstreperous of the grumblers and relied heavily on the small group of our colleagues who were supportive. Through the year, we organized an advisory system and planned a big extravaganza to launch the program. Regular classes were suspended and teachers offered special-interest classes to students—chess, puppet making, meditation, aerobics, singing for lousy singers, and the like. As was to be expected, a few of the teachers refused to do anything, saying they didn't have enough time to plan frivolous activities. Most we cajoled into doing something—leading walks, listening to music; those who claimed a lack of imagination ran study halls for those students who didn't want to participate in any of the other activities. The gala event having taken place, the house system was put into operation. Students reported to their advisory period for 1 hour per week.

As the year progressed, it became obvious to everyone that some teachers were growing to value the program; they'd say things to the administrators or to the four of us who were leading it. Those comments were sign enough of our success and, for the administrators, validation of their wisdom in creating the program. We did not know how the silent others were feeling, nor did we check. We were convinced that students liked the program because each of us had heard comments from some of our own students. In order to assess our efforts, the four of us teacher leaders and the administrators met at the end of the year. We congratulated ourselves on a job well done. We agreed that we would tighten up a few things the next year and proceed along the same path. I stayed in the school for several years, maintaining the leadership position in much the same way, and then moved on to a different school.

Several years ago, reports began stacking up on my university desk calling for teacher leadership positions. (See Carnegie, 1986; Holmes, 1986.) My interest was piqued and I read with enthusiasm—I didn't recall any such national cry previously but had long believed, based on my own experience and that of my colleagues, that teachers needed more powerful leadership roles in the improvement of education. Teachers are, after all, the ones who work daily with kids. And teachers' work, as it is currently organized, is not structured so that they might participate in the decision making about school improvement. Most schools and districts across the country are hierarchical places—places where the principal is vested with the decision-making power and authority in the school building. Principals set the schedule, allocate resources, determine who gets to go to which conferences, evaluate teachers, determine what will happen to the most problematic students, set the agenda for faculty meetings, and attend the board meetings on behalf of the school. A number of years ago, while teaching in a rural high school, I told the principal that I intended to go to the board meeting because board members were making curriculum decisions that would affect the work my students and I were doing. Within minutes, the superintendent marched into my room and told me in no uncertain terms that "his teachers" would not be attending his board meeting. He was not impressed when I reminded him that board meetings are public. And I, intimidated, did not go to the board meeting.

Teachers are distinguished one from the other not by their expertise or their particular contributions to students but by the salary schedule. The criteria used are the numbers of years in teaching and the number of degrees earned. Typically, all teachers hold equal status in the school and work in their own classrooms surrounded by youngsters all day long. Time for interaction with other adults is limited to the 20- to 30-minute lunch period, where there is often an unspoken code discouraging people from talking about work. A first-year teacher with whom I was working last year described how she learned about this code. She burst into her faculty room at lunchtime to share news of a lesson that had worked. (During almost all teachers' first year, this *is* cause for celebration!)

She was jubilant and couldn't share her lesson, how it had worked, and what the student had done fast enough. In mid-sentence she was interrupted by one of the informal leaders in the school. He said, "Listen. We come in here to relax. You can talk about the weather, the football scores, your lawn, your in-laws, dieting, your summer vacation—anything but work." Faculty meetings are the only other regular gathering of teachers. These generally involve listening to information from the principal rather than any kind of exchange. Teachers seldom have common planning periods or regularly scheduled time during the school year when they can work together to build or refine curriculum or to work on supporting individual students.

Professional growth is in large part determined and paid for by each individual teacher by attending college courses after school hours or during the summer in order to maintain current certification. A number of teachers attending a course I taught last summer described it as "credit collecting." Their interest was not in the course content but in getting the work done so that they could move up on the salary schedule. Another friend of mine, while describing the poor relationship between her college courses for an administrative certification and actual administrative work in schools, sarcastically described her professional growth experience as "buying a degree." Many teachers, of course, take courses that provide valuable methods for working with students. Still, in most schools there is no forum for teachers to share expertise gained in these courses with their colleagues, nor is there any arena at the university for teachers to influence the nature and the content of the courses. Thus, professional growth is frequently disconnected from the school and its aims for working with students.

Traditional leadership opportunities for teachers are extremely limited and generally serve an efficiency function rather than a leadership function. Classic definitions of leadership generally agree that "leaders" enable their colleagues to do things they wouldn't ordinarily do on their own to improve their professional practice. (See Bass, 1981.) Most leadership roles currently available are not designed to change practice but to ensure the efficiency and effectiveness of the existing system. Department heads in secondary schools provide a good example. In most cases department heads are responsible for coordinating the ordering of materials, for communicating the curricular requirements for the district and the state, and for competing for limited resources by getting to the principal before the other department heads. In some cases, department heads evaluate teachers in their department. No teachers I have interviewed have seen these positions as ones that enable them to learn and to grow. Nor do they build any kind of shared vision for the school. In elementary schools, teachers often head up textbook adoption committees. Their role is not to determine whether a textbook should be adopted or how they might change the structure of the curriculum so that kids learn more powerfully, but rather to engage their colleagues in the examination of texts and to select one. Although many teachers see this as an enormous responsibility because members of the committee become very invested in their particular choice of a basal reader, almost no teachers see committee work of this nature as influential in changing their instructional practices. Another common leadership role for teachers is union work. Participation in negotiations requires that teachers assemble their colleagues to talk about bread-and-butter issues—salaries, the calendar, sick leave, coaching responsibilities—but not about the school's goals for students, the graduation requirements, or the quality of instruction. It does, however, almost always place teachers in adversarial rather than collaborative relationships with their school board and administrators. Regular teachers in regular schools have little opportunity to influence or change set practice.

The new call for teacher leadership emerged from those dissatisfied with current conditions in education—policymakers, academicians, researchers—and is fueled by important and conclusive research conducted over the last 20 years that demonstrates that teachers, too long silent and isolated in classrooms, must take more leadership in the restructuring of public education. The powerful new rhetoric is undergirded by the belief that new leadership positions will improve the quality of educational experience students receive while simultaneously working to retain and to stretch top-quality people in the teaching profession. Descriptions of the possibilities recommend that teachers assume leadership in the redesign of the schools, mentor their colleagues, engage in problem solving at the school level, and provide professional growth opportunities for their colleagues. All of this was energizing for me; it jibed with my own experience in public education. Excited and hopeful, I began talking with colleagues, calling my teaching friends so that we could add to the list of new possibilities. Many of my school friends were less wildly enthusiastic than I. Some wilted at the thought of yet another bandwagon that promised to provide more work for teachers. Others gave me the phrase that always inspires instant cynicism in me, "Oh, we already do that." I ignored both these groups in favor of like-minded enthusiasts.

Sometime in the midst of our scheming, I was struck by the proverbial ton of bricks: These positions are not necessarily new. They have been around for years. They do exist in schools all across the country. The "we-already-doers" were right. I had held one! Although there hadn't been any significant national charge to build leadership positions for teachers at the time the position I had held was designed, the intentions behind that plan were similar—to improve the quality of public education while allowing teachers greater leadership in the development of those improvements. In addition, other friends of mine had been involved in mentoring efforts and in roles tailored to introduce new instructional techniques. These roles were, in fact, designed so that we could influence our colleagues to try new, more powerful practices with students.

As I sat considering my own experience in a teacher leadership position, a jumble of previously unexamined questions raced through my mind: Why did my art teacher friend cry, and why couldn't she be supportive when I was given the job? Who would she and the other complainers have selected given the chance? What kinds of positions would they have created, given the opportunity to discuss how they would go about improving the quality of educational experience for our students? How do actual teacher leaders feel about their positions? Do their positions make a difference for kids? Do they make a difference for their colleagues? Do these positions make teaching more challenging, more interesting? Why didn't we ever ask the other teachers in our building what they thought about the effectiveness of these leadership positions? What kind of diverse approaches exist among the teacher leadership positions that currently exist? Do some work better than others? What's the difference between the positions currently described in the reports and those that exist in practice?

Over a period of time during which I turned these questions around in my mind and with my colleagues, it seemed more and more reasonable to look closely at the teacher leadership roles that exist to see how they might inform the current rhetoric of reform. This book is my attempt to answer these questions, not by digging back into my own too distant past but by studying three teachers who currently hold leadership positions in their school districts in different parts of the country. Each of the teacher leaders holds a distinctly different kind of leadership role; each works at a different level of the K–12 system; each works in a different kind of educational setting; each of the roles is designed to enable teachers to examine new instructional practices so that they might improve their effectiveness with students. The purpose of this book is to better understand teacher leadership as it is now practiced in public schools. My belief is that current practice and its everyday, messy reality has great potential to inform and to strengthen the ongoing discussion of teacher leadership and educational improvement.

In order to explore the current rhetoric and the daily reality of teacher leaders, the book moves in the following way: Chapter 2 attempts to place the immediate discussion of teacher leadership in a sort of historical context. I briefly review the various, sometimes unrelated, strands of research that have led many people to the same conclusion that teachers need greater leadership opportunities if public education is to survive in any kind of meaningful way. Chapter 3 tells the story of Ted, a high school English teacher who runs an educational organization designed to create more powerful learning experiences for both teachers and students in addition to his half-time teaching position. Chapter 4 is the story of Gwen, an elementary teacher who is on half-time release in her own building to help her colleagues strengthen instruction. Chapter 5 contains Mary's story. Mary is a middle school teacher who created a demonstration classroom within her school in order to share new instructional strategies with her colleagues. Each of the case chapters includes a description of the teacher leader's working context, a portrait of the leader, a day-in-the-life sketch, interviews with their colleagues— those who were intended to have benefited from the leader's work— and a beginning examination of the case. Chapter 6 looks across the three cases to understand the supportive and constraining conditions of teacher leadership as it is practiced in these three roles and to identify major issues that emerge. Chapter 7 is an attempt to add a strengthening dose of reality to the rhetoric of reform. It begins with an outline of the problems and the paradoxes that exist in current teacher leadership roles, and continues with what I believe are some of the possibilities for reform and growth inherent in such leadership positions. The chapter closes with several fledgling images of teachers who lead—in newly formed roles, fragile but full of potential.

I chose to do three cases in the interest of depth over breadth. I recognize that there are hundreds, probably thousands of teacher leadership positions that exist around the country—all unique in some ways, each with its own strengths and weaknesses. I do not believe that these three are necessarily representative. (In Ted's case, the circumstances are in fact exceptional!) These stories do, however, represent a beginning, a glimpse at teacher leadership as it sounds, smells, and feels in schools on a normal day during the school year. They provide us with a sketchy framework upon which to build a more thorough examination of teacher leadership and its potential to strengthen our educational system for both the students and the adults in our schools.

CHAPTER 2

The Roots of Teacher Leadership

Because the discussion of teacher leadership is relatively new, no well-established body of literature traces the ideas that have produced the current cry for these positions. This chapter attempts to place the current emphasis in its recent historical context and then to demonstrate how the stories of three teacher leaders contribute to the conversation. The first part of this chapter reviews a number of studies done on a variety of topics that have led many people in educational circles to conclude that teachers must play a more active part in the restructuring of schools. The second section reviews the scant but important literature on teacher leadership. These studies clarify what is known about existing roles and illustrate what remains to be investigated. The third brief section describes the organization of the stories of three teacher leaders presented in the following chapters. The review here is a beginning attempt to place the teacher leadership discussion in its context. It is by no means definitive, and much has been written on the subject since I completed this study. (See, e.g., Smylie & Denny, 1989; Fay, 1990; Miller, 1990.)

PART I: WORKING CONDITIONS IN TEACHING

Teaching has long been described as a bleak profession, as made obvious in the irritating old maxim, "Those that can't, teach." The following studies document problematic working conditions within teaching. In the tradition established by Waller (1961) in the 1930s, Lortie (1975) outlines the history of the teaching profession in the United States. Teaching is characterized by haphazard recruitment, preparation programs that don't match the realities of practice, a sink-or-swim entry into the profession, and extreme isolation from other adults. In addition, teaching is full of uncertainties. It is difficult for teachers to determine whether they have been successful. More often than not, curricular goals are unclear and left to the individual. Relationships are also confusing. Parent-teacher relations are generally strained. Teacher-administrator relations are strained in some places. Teacher-board relations are frequently nonexistent and confusing where they do exist. In addition, the teaching career is flat, with little opportunity to change working conditions or professional opportunities unless one chooses to leave teaching altogether to go into administration.

Lieberman and Miller (1984) researched the complexities of teaching by describing the dailiness of practice at the elementary and secondary levels. At both levels, teachers face 5 or 6 hours with students, little or no opportunity to work with other adults, the constant demand to be practical in the face of hundreds of daily decisions, and the crippling uncertainty about their personal effectiveness. Elementary teachers face problems of curriculum overload, the lack of coordination from grade level to grade level, and the necessity to deal with students from diverse backgrounds and at different levels of readiness. Secondary teachers work in highly bureaucratic systems where they compete—department to department—for limited resources. They encounter huge numbers of students every day who bring with them the same range of experience and preparedness as do students in elementary schools.

McLaughlin, Wallin, Pfeifer, Swanson-Owens, and Yee (1986) discuss the results of interviews with teachers conducted to find out how they do, in fact, measure their own efficacy. The study concludes that "in fundamental ways, the U.S. educational system is structured to guarantee the failure of teachers' (p. 420). Teachers find it impossible to foster the growth and development of students for a variety of reasons. The clientele is conscripted, and teachers have little or no control over the way things are done. They have too many students and inadequate resources, in addition to all of the problems isolated by Lortie (1969, 1975) and by Lieberman and Miller (1984). The result is that they are unable to meet their own goals—improving learning for students—and the effects of this are devastating.

Twenty years later, Cohn, Kottcamp, McCloskey, and Provenzo (1987) studied the same teachers who had participated in Lortie's Five Cities study. The researchers were interested to know whether teachers perceived the problems in their profession to be the same as those indicated in the recent reports, and whether conditions in general had changed since the earlier study. Teachers indicated that three key factors proved the most troublesome: (1) the changing attitude of students and parents, (2) the changing nature of the profession, and (3) long-standing low salaries. Teachers find both parents and students to be far more unwilling partners than in the past. Changing family structures, drugs, television, urbanization—all contribute to students' lack of motivation and parents' uncooperative support of the schools. Teachers' work has become less professional, more bureaucratic. Teachers are no longer able to make decisions in the best interests of their students because they are confronted by more external control, more paperwork, less time for planning and teaching, less involvement in curricular decisions, and little control over student assessment issues. Teachers perceive that their status has changed and that they no longer command the respect the profession once held.

Again, low salaries, which have always been problematic, persist in causing teachers to take on second jobs and, in many cases, to leave the profession. Sykes (1987) investigated the incentives in teaching. Because teachers work in isolation, there is no system for promotion in the teaching career, and salaries are low, incentives are extremely weak. Weak incentives promote high rates of turnover, keep costs down, allow for low commitment, and free teachers to look for external rewards outside of teaching—summer jobs, other sideline occupations. Sykes (1987) contends that the conditions created by weak incentives contribute to the poor quality of education that exists today. He notes that if incentives for teachers come mainly from their students, the structure of rewards needs to be reconfigured to ensure greater student success. Such consideration has not been evident in previous attempts to strengthen the teaching profession.

Social Changes and Teacher Shortages

Another research focus that has implications for teacher leadership deals with teacher shortages. Although teacher shortages have historically been a cyclical phenomenon in public education, Darling-Hammond (1984) illustrated that the profession currently faces a shortage of major proportion, due to a number of social changes (see

also Sykes, 1983). Because women and minorities have made significant gains in entry to nontraditional occupations, fewer and fewer are
selecting teaching. As salaries rise in other professions and remain
low in teaching, fewer young people are choosing to teach. A major
proportion of the teaching work force is nearing retirement age. As
more teachers retire, fewer people are choosing to enter the profession. Many states responded to these predictions by conducting their
own studies on potential shortages (see, e.g., Theobald, 1987) that
reinforce the findings described by Darling-Hammond. Fears of a
major teacher shortage heighten the need for the discussion of
teacher leadership as the necessity to attract and retain good teachers
becomes ever more pressing.

The Complexity of Change

Several classic works demonstrate the complexity involved in
changing schools. The Rand Studies (Berman & McLaughlin, 1978)
investigated the effects of federal programs funded to bring about
badly needed change in the public schools. The findings indicated
that the difference between success and failure in these programs
depended on how well the local school district implemented the
program. In addition, few of the programs lasted in important ways
once the federal funds dried up. The authors indicated that although
implementation and funding were critical factors, problems articulated at the federal level and time lines generated for the implementation of solutions were generally oversimplified and, thus, confounded the original intentions of the programs.

Sarason (1971) wrote an important book entitled *The Culture of
the School and the Problem of Change* that is remarkably pertinent
today. The author describes two types of regularities that are affected
by change but are seldom given adequate consideration: (1) programmatic and (2) behavioral. Programmatic regularities are found in the
schedule—a six-period day, in isolated subjects—English, math,
science. Behavioral regularities are illustrated when teachers lecture
to students, and when they test for knowledge retention. Behavioral
and programmatic regularities seldom match the intended outcomes,
what we hope for in schools. For instance, many educators want
students to be powerful communicators yet establish few opportunities for them to practice communication skills. Unfortunately, efforts

made in the interest of change seldom encourage the kind of planning and support that would make it possible to match the regularities of schooling to the intended outcomes.

Cuban (1988) asks an important question: How it can be that American schools have been involved in reform almost constantly throughout the last century, and yet schools look so much the same? He concludes that school reformers have attempted two kinds of changes: First-order changes are quality-control issues—changes that deal with improving the efficiency and the effectiveness of the existing system. The underlying assumption is that the existing system is good and should be maintained—if modified. Second-order changes are ones of design that require significant restructuring of the existing system. Cuban believes that first-order changes have been fairly successful in American schools, whereas second-order reforms have met with little success because of flawed implementation and inadequate planning. He notes that if serious changes for teachers and students are critical, then it is second-order changes that need to be addressed.

Popkewitz, Tabachnick, and Wehlage (1982) studied the 4-year implementation of a federally developed program that was intended to produce comprehensive school reform. They found three types of schools: (1) technical schools, which adopted the curricular program in its totality and focused on following implementation plans exactly as specified; (2) constructive schools, which adopted the parts of the program that complemented their existing programs; and (3) illusory schools, which adopted the language, the posters, and wore the buttons but changed nothing in their classrooms. The authors concluded that any reform effort involves teachers' and administrators' underlying assumptions about knowledge, their concepts of teachers' working responsibilities, and their personal ideologies. Unless these underlying assumptions are dealt with, no real reform takes place.

These works together make clear that the success and the failure of reform attempts depend heavily on local school personnel. Traditional reforms have been created by outsiders who oversimplify the complexity of the change process, who do not engage in thorough planning, and who short-circuit implementation plans. These findings have directly influenced the discussion of teacher leadership by demonstrating that teachers must be involved in the restructuring of their careers and their working conditions if results are to be achieved.

The American Classroom Experience

High School (Boyer, 1983), *Horace's Compromise* (Sizer, 1984), and *A Place Called School* (Goodlad, 1984) were very important studies that examined what life is like for both students and teachers in classrooms. Boyer, after investigating 15 high schools across the country, determined that:

> The working conditions of teachers must improve. Many people think teachers have soft, undemanding jobs. The reality is different. Teachers are expected to work miracles day after day and then often get only silence from the students, pressure from the principals, and criticism from the irate parent. (p. 307)

Findings from this study indicated that teachers' basic working conditions were abysmal and antithetical to the promotion of good learning for students. He recommended that work loads be cut to four classes and that teachers be given longer preparatory time, duty-free noninstructional time, and more opportunities to pursue interest areas related to teaching. The report contained recommendations for a career path for teachers. "Two of the most troublesome aspects of the teaching profession today are the lack of a career ladder and the leveling off of salaries. The irony is that to 'get ahead' in teaching, you must leave it" (Boyer, 1983, p. 310).

Goodlad's (1984) study was the first large-scale investigation of actual classroom work. Observations of 1,350 teachers were conducted in 1,000 classrooms from the full range of K–12 levels. He found that schools are routinized places where teachers use the least effective teaching methods to convey information that has been oversimplified and, as a result, made lifeless. In addition, the findings describe a system that does not provide equal opportunities or equal access to knowledge for all students. Practices such as ability-tracking encourage the teachers to deliver the best instruction, and the more interesting curriculum, to the most academically able students, whereas both the quality of instruction and the expectations for student performance diminish through the lower tracks. These findings caused widespread discussion about actual classroom practices and challenged what had long been considered accepted norms in teaching.

Sizer's (1984) work outlines the paradox in which most teachers find themselves. In the course of his investigation in secondary schools, he describes Horace, a hypothetical English teacher caught between his students, the existing structure, the curriculum, the administration, and the parents. Horace faces overloaded curriculum, too many students, and a system that encourages order as opposed to engagement. He finds himself caught between knowing what his students really need and the existing educational system that encourages the kind of instruction his students need least. The irony in this paradox is crushing. He compromises his best professional judgment in order to remain what he wants most to be—a teacher—and watches his students remain passive and disengaged.

These studies focused on actual classroom practices generated some very powerful themes: Instruction is flat, disjointed, and aimed at coverage rather than at learning. Teachers use only a fraction of the known instructional methods available to them. Students of differing ability levels have very different kinds of school experiences—experiences that are unequal in a system designed to provide equal opportunity for all. Such findings brought the need for significant changes in all aspects of teaching to light. Teacher training, teacher in-service education, teacher work conditions, the structure of the teaching career, all emerged as very important issues in the restructuring of public education.

First-Wave Reforms and the Effects on Teaching

Yet another group of studies focuses on what is now called the first wave of reform and its effects on teaching. The first wave began with the appearance of the Reagan administration's report, *A Nation at Risk*, and the economic policy that gave responsibility for school funding back to individual states. In response, legislatures across the country developed their own reports on the conditions of schooling in their state, and mandated school improvement and heightened accountability as a means by which to ensure better quality public education. A report by Wise (1979) predicted from the outset of the movement that legislated learning would not improve the quality of public schooling. He foresaw that centralized regulation would prohibit teachers from responding to the real diversity that exists in their student population.

Almost 10 years later, a study conducted by McCloskey, Porvenzo, Cohen, and Kottcamp (1987) confirmed Wise's predictions. Both Wise's earlier work and this analysis indicate that teaching in a highly regulated system hardly allows for professional judgment and that working conditions in these circumstances promote a tell-me-what-to-do mentality (see also Wise, 1988).

McNeil (1986) scrutinized legislated learning and its impact on classroom instruction. McNeil's study documents that central bureaucratization of schools places greater emphasis on control than on learning. As a result, teachers find themselves using defensive teaching methods as a means of controlling students in order to comply with the valued norms established in a hierarchical system—quiet, tidy classrooms. Defensive teaching includes omitting essential but controversial subject matter from the curriculum or fragmenting and mystifying difficult topics in order to avoid conflict and disruption. These techniques contribute to, rather than protect against, the poor quality of student learning.

These studies demonstrate again that legislated learning suggested by those who do not work in schools has unintended consequences that cancel the good intentions of the hopeful reformers. As the consequences of mandated change are more clearly understood in light of the effects on teachers and students, the search for ways to involve teachers becomes more critical.

Is Teaching a Profession?

All of the work mentioned previously reopened the discussion on the nature of professionalism and its relationship to teaching (see, e.g., Darling-Hammond, 1988; Sykes, 1987; Soder, 1986). Definitions of "professional" practice commonly agree that professionals develop a specialized knowledge base from which appropriate decisions can be made on behalf of clients; that professionals have the ability to apply that knowledge in individual, nonroutine circumstances; and that they have a strong ethical commitment to do what is best for the client. In addition, according to common definitions, professionals usually work together to determine the requirements of credentialing and licensure.

Current research illustrates that it is difficult to describe teaching using these definitions. Teachers work in bureaucratic systems that discourage decision making at the classroom level. Teachers seldom have the opportunity to work together on professional issues. Teachers do not determine the standards against which they are judged, nor do they determine the standards against which their students should be measured. Clark (1987) notes that these circumstances do not serve anyone's purposes very well. "Contemporary organizations have sacrificed the freedom of their employees in favor of control over those employees to the disadvantage of both the employee and the organization" (p. 1).

Shulman (1983) pushes the conundrum further by describing the tension between autonomy and obligation. Teachers need autonomy to make appropriate decisions for their students, whereas policymakers feel the obligation to ensure quality control to their constituents—the population at large. It is this essential paradox that has led many educational experts to attempt to clarify who, in the process of schooling, has the professional responsibility for which decisions.

Kerr (1987) clarifies what she believes to be the lines of responsibility for decision making from the political arena to the classroom door. She notes that policymakers at the state level have the responsibility to ensure adequate resources, to guarantee equitable distribution of public education, and to provide broad guidelines describing the general aims of schooling. Teachers and principals have political, moral, and epistemic responsibility to their clients/students to encourage the belief that all can learn. In addition, she indicates that teachers and principals must take responsibility for students' learning by questioning the efficacy of their efforts.

Goodlad (1987a) argues that schools are, like the natural environment, ecological systems where decisions made at any level affect all other levels. As a result, he indicates, schools must be centers of renewal, places of critical inquiry where teachers and principals have primary decision-making responsibility in order to foster best learning in children. He notes that principals and teachers must have the authority to make and then modify the educational program so that they can best respond to the needs of their particular student clientele.

Sirotnik (1987b) contends that schools have been driven by the kinds of evaluations that have been conducted to measure student success. In recent years, these evaluations have shown an unhealthy

reverence for scientific management. Such evaluations have traditionally focused on the necessity to locate measurable outcomes, to
evaluate product rather than process, and to ensure objectivity so that
judgment about school efficacy becomes tests developed and scored
from outside the school. Sirotnik believes that if schools are to
engage in serious renewal, the people who work in schools must be
the ones to check their own efficacy, that this is part of their
professional responsibility. To do this, teachers and principals must
constantly gather information about their own professional practices
to determine what works and what does not. That information must
be combined with current knowledge about teaching and learning so
that the staff can make informed decisions. Finally, the staff must
rigorously evaluate the consequences of the decisions made. Such
schools would provide teachers with the kind of professional autonomy they have long needed to improve the quality of education.

Shulman (1987) notes that current practices in education miss
professional definitions in another way. He states that within the
existing system, knowledge about teaching is currently generated
from outside the teaching profession itself. Developed by university
faculty and educational researchers, the knowledge base has moved,
because of its roots in empirical research, toward prescriptive teaching. Knowledge generated in this way oversimplifies the complexities of practice and fails to take into account the wisdom of practice
cultivated by practitioners.

To summarize, in the existing hierarchical system, teachers do
not have the capability to make professional decisions in the best
interest of their students. Nor have they developed their own knowledge base. Nor have teachers worked together to determine the
standards for credentialing or for measuring the efficacy of their
work. These conditions cripple teachers' capacity to improve schools
on behalf of student learning.

The Benefits of Collegiality

Several researchers involved in the discussion about how best to
improve schools have seen collaboration and collegiality as the means
by which to facilitate positive change. Lieberman (1985-86, 1986,
1987, 1988a, 1988b, 1988c) drew on many of the studies previously
cited as she articulated the critical need for collaboration. Collabora-

tive relationships are needed between and among all members of the educational endeavor if schools are to be restructured in significant ways.

Little (1986) documented the power of collegiality for the first time. She detailed the everyday behaviors of principals who made collegial practice a norm in their buildings. In these schools, characterized by collegiality and experimentation, teachers worked with the principal to set realistic goals and to share leadership. Principals made sure that people practiced the skills required for collaborative work, encouraged experimentation, and provided time for staff members to work together.

Rosenholtz (1989) provided the first link between school structure and teacher growth. In order to find out how teacher growth takes place, she conducted research in several school districts. Schools characterized as "learning enriched" were places where there were collaborative goals set at the building level, where there was a minimum of uncertainty and a maximum of shared positive attitudes. In these schools, principals supported teachers by removing the roadblocks to change and fostered collaboration as opposed to competition. In "learning-impoverished schools" there were neither clear goals nor shared values, nor time to interact with colleagues. Teachers described these schools as routine. Teachers in learning-impoverished schools claimed that it takes 3 to 4 years to become good teachers. Teachers in learning-enriched schools claimed that it takes a lifetime. Engaged in constant discussion about their work, these teachers better understood the complexity involved in teaching.

McLaughlin and Yee (1988) studied 85 teachers to determine what makes a satisfying teaching career. One of the major findings in the study dealt with the benefits of collegiality. Whereas the traditional definition of a good career is based on a vertical configuration—advancement, success, and reward structures—teachers view a good career in individual terms. Their notion depends more on personal meanings. Teachers look for ways to grow professionally rather than ways to ascend a hierarchical ladder; success to them means increasing effectiveness with students, not another rung up that ladder. Further, McLaughlin and Yee found that schools that support a good teaching career are places that foster collegiality, instructional integration, and problem solving as opposed to problem hiding or ignoring.

Lieberman and Rosenholtz (1987) discussed the dualities inherent in the creation of such collaborative schools: standardization versus diversity, autonomy versus obligation, bureaucratization versus professionalization, management by control versus the facilitation of professional norms, and mandatory versus voluntary change. Clearly, the creation of such new settings challenges much of the traditional organizational structure.

These studies indicate that teacher growth and change thrive in an environment where the school community shares values and goals, where teachers are provided the time to reflect and to work together, where people are taught how to work collaboratively, and where they are focused on issues of curriculum and instruction—the greatest concerns of teachers.

The Call for Teacher Leadership: Second-Wave Reform Reports

Issues raised in many of the studies mentioned above were discussed in two very influential reports, frequently called the second-wave reform reports. These reports, influenced by the research previously cited, made strong and powerful recommendations for teacher leadership. The first, titled *Teachers for the 21st Century* (Carnegie, 1986), recommends that schools create more professional environments to include professional autonomy for teachers, lead teacher positions, time for professional development, and deregulation so that school-site staff have greater opportunities to participate in the decisions affecting their schools.

The Carnegie Commission charged Devaney (1987) with the task of developing a more thorough description of what teacher leadership should do and what it might look like. Devaney called for new roles that would professionalize the whole occupation, would empower other teachers, and would allow teachers to become architects of school reform. Such roles might include mentoring of beginning teachers; appraising and critiquing performance to foster individual growth; designing, organizing, and conducting staff in-service; and facilitating reviews of building-level concerns. She noted that continuation of classroom practice should be considered when designing these roles, and that potential roles should be planned with an eye to the surrounding context to determine how these roles might affect everyone else. Devaney also observed that existing leadership roles seem to be riddled with problems and ineffectual in bringing about significant change.

The second major report, *Tomorrow's Teachers* (Holmes Group, 1986), recommended closer collaboration between practitioners and university faculty in the improvement of teacher training and continued teacher education and for the development of a three-tiered career ladder for teachers that would include role differentiation between beginning teachers, professional teachers, and career professionals.

Both of these reports drew national attention to teaching and, more specifically, made a strong case for the need for more various roles for teachers and for more professional opportunities during the teaching career. These reports suggested role differentiation following patterns already well established in business. The assumptions were that these new kinds of leadership roles for teachers would strengthen the incentives to join or to stay in the profession, would reduce teacher isolation, and would build better models for teacher training and for continued teacher growth.

Implications for Teacher Leadership

Each of these groups of studies, although focused on different ends, arrive at similar conclusions. Each group illustrates a particular aspect of the larger educational canvas: One highlights students sitting passively in the classroom, another shows a teacher working over the years in isolation from other adults, another shows a legislator handing down a decree to teachers. Taken as a whole, the picture is very clear: Teaching in its current state is problematic and unlikely to produce more competent students in the years to come. Changes are desperately needed if teachers are to be able to contribute to the revitalization of schools. Unless these changes are made, it is likely that more good teachers will leave the system, while fewer new candidates decide to participate; thus, the teacher shortage will reach even greater proportions than is now expected. There appears to be a growing consensus that teachers must be involved in the restructuring of their own profession, and such participation demands new leadership roles for teachers.

In places where principals and teachers have begun to chip away at the existing system, they have been able to reduce teacher isolation and to encourage greater educational experimentation in the hope that teachers might seriously begin to participate in the improvement of their own schools. These newly emerging settings require that everyone in the educational endeavor function differently and more collaboratively, again indicating that teachers must play a stronger leadership role in the reshaping of schools.

The discussion to this point establishes the need for teacher leadership but does not describe in any detail what that might be or how it might be done. Nor does it suggest in any concrete ways how these new, hypothetical roles differ from those that teachers have held for years.

PART II: RESEARCH ON TEACHER LEADERSHIP

Leadership roles have been in place for the last century—head teachers, department chairs, master teachers. In recent years a few new roles have emerged—team leaders, curriculum developers, and staff-development trainers, to mention just a few. The scant mention of these roles in the discussions about teacher leadership would lead one to assume that current positions are not providing the kinds of rejuvenation that are perceived necessary. However, it does seem likely that the study of the existing roles will reveal information helpful in understanding the distinction between what is needed and what exists.

A small body of recent literature on teacher leadership as it currently exists includes surveys and case studies of particular leadership roles. These works clarify what is known and what remains to be explored.

Devaney based her beliefs about existing roles on a study done by Hatfield, Blackman, Claypool, and Master (1987). The authors attempted to investigate several areas: (1) to identify the people who hold these roles, (2) to describe their activities and responsibilities, (3) to develop a description of the organizational conditions that support these roles. Their findings indicated that 10% to 20% of the teaching staff was represented by more than 50 titles. The newest roles are master teachers, grade-level chairs, and staff-development specialists. The oldest roles are consultants and department chairs. Release time was provided to less than 35%, whereas compensation in some form was provided to some 63%. Teachers in these roles tended to hold multiple assignments, to lack concrete job descriptions, to be given the positions by administrative appointment, and to lack training.

The teachers studied identified the following skills and qualities as important to their work: the ability to deal with people, to communicate well, to be flexible and patient, to be competent, and to be well respected. Teachers surveyed noted that relations with principals were often difficult and that they lacked a power base or any formal authority. Although a majority of their work concentrated on staff development, curricular development, and instructional improvement, the more focused the role, the more successful it appeared. The authors concluded that despite extensive use of these roles, they have not surfaced as significant.

In order to add to the information gained in the Hatfield et al. (1987) study, I worked with teachers in 13 school districts to design and carry out a study of what teacher leadership looks like in the northwestern part of the United States (Dierks et al., 1988). The purpose was to determine whether the roles teachers held locally were more permanent or, as Hatfield's study suggested, impermanent and largely unrecognized. We wanted to see whether the work these leaders did was focused on curricular and instructional issues or on administrative issues, and whether teachers in leadership positions believed that there should be more opportunities for leadership.

Findings from interviews conducted with 87 teachers indicated that a good deal of their responsibility required committee meetings, and that relatively little of their time was spent working with other teachers on issues related to instruction. Many of the roles these people held were informal and voluntary, whereas 62% indicated that they received some form of reward. Of that 62%, 55% indicated extrinsic rewards—lighter teaching loads, release time, extra stipends—whereas the others indicated intrinsic rewards—personal satisfaction, resumé building, greater influence—constituted their primary compensation. When asked to indicate what changes are needed for teachers to function as leaders, most teachers agreed with the following comment, which illustrates the major theme: "Time seems to be the fulcrum on which better teaching rests. More time for collaboration among teachers was the most frequent request for change among teacher leaders. Currently, direct teacher to teacher contact for the purpose of improving classroom instruction is rare" (Dierks et al., 1988, p. 13).

In addition, those interviewed indicated that they needed access to information that is difficult to obtain in hierarchical systems, that they needed leadership training, and that they needed more knowledge in areas of budget and finance, school law, multicultural education, current educational research, change processes, and participatory decision-making processes.

Several other studies focused on particular kinds of teacher leadership roles. Because of their narrowed perspective, these studies tell us a great deal about the benefits and the problems with such roles. Porter (1986) investigated the effects of a leadership role developed out of a collaboration between teachers and Michigan State University's Institute for Reasearch on Teaching (IRT). The university wished to bridge the traditional gap between classroom practice and university-based research. Five teachers were selected through an application process to work half-time at the university for an average period of 3 years.

Porter found that the benefits of such collaborations were significant for the teachers involved. Specifically, they reported greater intellectual stimulation, reduced isolation, the distance to become analytical about their practice, and an increase in both their personal confidence and their commitment to the profession. On the other hand, teachers also reported that the job split between their school and the university was stressful, that they did not have enough time to do all that was required in both workplaces, and that administrators in their school systems paid very little attention to their university-based work. One participant noted:

> My days with the Institute for Research on Teaching have been privileged ones, allowing me to see how research and teaching can nourish one another. My years here, however, have shown me that in spite of my best efforts and personal successes in combining research and classroom teaching, they remain separate territories with well defined boundaries. I have not been able to bring them together for anyone other than myself. That's a shame. (p. 16)

Finally, teachers in this study reported a tremendous difficulty in reentering the classroom full-time after completing their work at the IRT. Porter's study provides a snapshot of one leadership position that seems to have strong personal benefits for those involved, but that does not spread benefits to the larger teaching force.

Lieberman, Saxi, and Miles (1988) studied 17 teachers in the New York school system who held extended positions in individual school buildings. Their study focused on what people did when they assumed newly created leadership positions designed to assist other teachers. These positions were formal in that they were negotiated between the teachers' union and the administration. Selection was done by the union. Teachers who won the positions were on full-time release and were assigned to a single building. They were not assigned to buildings in which they had taught previously.

The authors found that all of those who were selected worked in a variety of ways. The jobs were partially created by the school context and, as a result, the leaders found it necessary to learn a variety of leadership skills while on the job. Because they had not worked collaboratively before, the teacher leaders were able to isolate several categories of skills they needed to be effective with their colleagues. The leadership skills they felt they needed were:

1. Trust and rapport building
2. Organizational diagnosis
3. Dealing with process
4. Managing the work
5. Building skill and confidence in others

Characteristics of these new roles included the necessity of placing nonjudgmental value on providing assistance, on modeling collegiality as a mode of work, on making provisions for continual learning, and on encouraging others to take leadership with their peers. The benefits of these positions ranged from improving the self-esteem of those who held the roles to building stronger school-based support groups and networks.

Little (1987) evaluated the likelihood of the success of teacher leadership roles. She indicated that it is impossible to professionalize teaching without dealing with three major problems:

1. Conditions of membership
2. Structure of the teaching career
3. Conditions of productivity in schools

According to Little, career ladder plans under consideration in many places in the country are unlikely to attract and retain excellent teachers because the rewards are not significant enough to affect many candidates. Such plans oversimplify the complexity of organizational problems facing teachers in that they do not provide more time for teachers to work together. Furthermore, teachers have not been significantly involved in the creation of these roles to take them seriously, nor is it likely that they will respond to role differentiation after such a long history of egalitarian status. She noted that teachers who hold extended positions often lead alone—because no one follows.

Autonomy—which is viewed as freedom from outside scrutiny and the right to make independent judgments—historically has been a very strong standard of practice. Every teacher knows the old saying about being able to do anything once the classroom door is closed. The norms of privacy within the teaching profession are so strong that it is not clear how readily teachers will accept advice or growth experiences designed by another teacher. Little determined that in order for teacher leadership roles to be successful, the following conditions must exist:

1. The work leaders do must be significant.
2. They must not be symbolic roles for "hit" people, who will attempt to remove less able teachers.
3. The roles must have clear ground rules.
4. The incentives and rewards must be clear.
5. There must be local policy support.
6. Teacher leaders must have good training.
7. The roles must be supported within the professional organizations or unions.

Given this list of considerations, Little concluded that it is unlikely that teacher leadership will succeed as it is currently being conceived by would-be reformers. In a more recent work (Little, 1988), she noted that there are high costs to working collaboratively—time and conflict. These, too, are obstacles to teacher leadership.

These studies indicate that teachers are interested in new opportunities to expand their skills and involvement. Those who hold leadership positions seem to benefit from them and would like to see the possibilities expanded. All said that they developed whole new skills as a result of their attempts to influence their colleagues.

At the same time, a number of problems surface. Many noted that their work was administrative rather than focused on instruction. They lacked training. The existing conditions in teaching did not provide security for leadership roles. There are high costs in terms of time and conflict. There is little evidence that these roles support those they were designed to serve and little evidence that they improve the quality of educational experience their students received.

Unanswered Questions

At this point, the works reviewed in Part I of this chapter substantiate the need for such positions but do not describe what those roles might look like in any concrete way. The fact that the roles mentioned in the reports are positions that already exist in various school districts around the country is confusing. Many school people dismiss the discussion as another example of policymakers' lack of understanding about what really happens in schools. As a result, school people are more inclined to ignore the conversation and carry on—school as usual—without feeling the need to examine the roles that exist much further, an unacceptable circumstance if, as almost everyone agrees, school improvement and new roles for teachers are really needed.

The few studies done on existing leadership positions illustrate both problems and benefits, and raise a number of unanswered questions. Do the leadership roles that exist provide growth opportunities and incentives for more than a limited few? What kinds of roles would teachers who are not in leadership positions create? How do teachers who are supposed to benefit from a leader's efforts feel about the positions? Is there any evidence that the existing roles improve the quality of educational experience for students? How is evaluation of existing roles conducted? How do the teacher organizations and unions feel about the kinds of roles teachers currently hold? Is the work more focused on administrative planning than on issues that would strengthen classroom teaching? Is selection done primarily by administrators? Given the option, would teachers select colleagues for leadership positions? How does the context affect these roles? Does the context shape the role, or can roles be exported from one place to another? These questions echoed those that had plagued me earlier and forced me to begin thinking about how I might find some answers. My central purpose was to observe three different teacher leaders at work to better understand the difference between the current national cry for teacher leadership positions and those that currently exist in practice.

PART III: THE CASES

Ted, Mary, and Gwen are three teachers who hold leadership positions within their own settings in different parts of the United States. They represent only a tiny sample of the leadership roles currently held by nearly 10% of the teaching force across the country (Hatfield et al., 1987). During 2 weeks I spent with each of them, I looked for answers to the questions that had emerged from my own experience as a teacher leader and from reading about teacher leadership in the current discussion. The questions became more focused as I arrived at the schoolhouse doors: What is the nature of the work teacher leaders do? What are the constraints? What are the conditions that support these positions? How do the teachers who hold these positions define teacher leadership? How do their colleagues define it? How are these people selected and evaluated for these positions? Does the association support them? Do their fellow teachers find these roles to be helpful to their own instruction, their own professional growth? Do these roles make the teaching career more interesting so that good teachers are both attracted to the profession and provided with enough incentives to stay? Do the roles encourage greater experimentation and collegiality among the larger teaching force? Do they provide more powerful learning for students?

Each of the cases provides some preliminary answers to these questions. Collectively, they offer some exploratory insights into the nature of teacher leadership roles in general, and provoke some deeper thinking with which to respond to the current call for more powerful leadership experiences for teachers.

Organization of the Case Studies

Each of the cases is organized in several parts. The first part, titled "The Context," describes the schools and the culture in which the teacher leaders work. The second describes the major subject and is labeled "The Person." A day-in-the-life sketch of each of the subjects follows to give readers some sense of the scope, the flow, and the pace of the work of the teacher leaders. Each of the sketches includes after-school meetings; although meetings were common, those represented did not occur every day. The next section, titled "Other Responsibilities," describes those activities that were an important part of the teacher leader's work, but that were not part of each day. The following section summarizes the conversations I had with the teacher leader's colleagues. Finally, I examine each case individually to understand better how it defines teacher leadership and then highlight the dominant themes that emerge.

CHAPTER 3

TED NEWTON
An Entrepreneurial Teacher

*I don't fill any leadership role. I'm not saying that to be modest.
It's true. I'm not—I don't have a leadership role in the English
department and I don't have a leadership role among the faculty
itself. . . . I just teach like everybody else.*

—*Ted Newton*

THE CONTEXT

Ted works in a small, conservative, southern, rural community. He
teaches in the local public high school and is the president of a
corporation formed out of his work with students. He is in his 22nd
year of teaching. Talking Mountain is the name of the corporation
that sponsors courses for teachers, coordinates networks of teachers
who teach according to the Talking Mountain philosophy, and produces materials—tape recordings, magazines, curriculum guides,
radio shows, and books—written and developed by high school students and/or the Talking Mountain staff. That philosophy, heavily
influenced by John Dewey, promotes experiential education for students so that their school life is more closely connected to the world
in which they live. The college-level courses Ted teaches for educators
are offered at a number of universities in different parts of the
country, mostly in the summer. Teachers who have taken the course
are then invited to participate in a network of like-minded teachers
and are provided with financial and collegial support as they work to
experiment with the Talking Mountain experiential education philosophy. The corporation has obtained grants that provide teachers

30

with small sums of money to facilitate their classroom experiments. In addition, the corporation produces a curriculum magazine for teachers that features articles written by teachers within the networks, explaining their projects. Each of their projects experiments with the instructional philosophy.

Ted's personal experience and work with students at the local high school led him to publish a magazine of local culture. The magazine, begun 22 years ago, recorded the ways, crafts, and traditions of the local mountain community. Because of the unique stories the students published, selections from the magazine turned into a number of best-selling books. The students did all the manuscript preparation, tracked the editing process, and dealt with their subjects in the same way anthropologists do. The royalties from the books allowed Ted and his students to form the corporation and to expand their activities within the public school. As a result, Talking Mountain provides salaries for nine full-time employees, five of whom are certified teachers and three of whom teach courses at the local high school according to the Talking Mountain philosophy. Ted teaches four courses during the regular school year, one of which produces the magazine, which is sent to subscribers in all of the 50 states and several foreign countries. Another prepares students for the magazine production course. The other two are college preparatory English courses that are part of the regular high school curriculum. The Talking Mountain staff offers another 11 classes at the high school, coordinates the teacher networks, develops curriculum guides that they are writing with their students, and facilitates the production of the audio- and videotapes that the students are also doing. In essence, the arrangement here is a sort of school within a school, or a curriculum enhancement program. Ted provides additional staff to the school district, and a richer curriculum as a result, in exchange for the opportunity to work with high school students.

The Talking Mountain staff has also formed a kind of exchange with the community, dignifying local culture and history and involving community members in a number of their activities and as the primary sources for their work. For instance, Talking Mountain purchased 110 acres of land on a mountainside. Ted, his students, and community members bought some old log buildings and relocated them onto the property during the summer months, taking care to restore them with historical accuracy. Some of the buildings house the Talking Mountain offices. Within others, they have catalogued a huge collection of local artifacts and antiques. Yet another is an old blacksmith's shop where students can learn to make nails, to pound horseshoes, and to keep farm implements in good shape. The staff, community members, and students are presently engaged in creating authentic turn-of-the-century mountain gardens and collecting local wildflowers. Talking Mountain also has a board of local community members who advise the organization on its work in the community.

The school system in which all this innovation has taken place is the epitome of traditional. The hierarchy of authority is clearly defined: The superintendent and school board make decisions that are in keeping with the conservative community. Those decisions foster the maintenance of public schooling as it has existed in the United States since the turn of the century—one teacher, one class-room, one textbook for each student. The principal functions as a monitor of the board's directives and, as a result, spends the bulk of his time managing the school. In my brief interactions with him (during which time he addressed me as both "Shug" (short for sugar) and "Little Lady" in a thick southern drawl), he was not concerned with or involved in any discussions to reform or improve schools. He accepted the traditional system and focused his energy to make sure that it worked well. He was conscientious, hardworking, and believed that he and his staff were doing the very best they could for the local students. In keeping with his strong sense of the importance of the traditional system, he neither promoted nor denigrated Ted's pro-grams. He behaved toward Ted as to any other staff member, recently writing Ted up for not having coded his lesson plans to the state standards on time.

The district allows Ted to work within its system, as long as nothing he does requires special consideration from them. As a result, all of the Talking Mountain staff members are certified teachers, evaluated by the principal and the vice principal, and subject to the same kinds of responsibilities as the rest of the staff but paid by Talking Mountain. The dominant relationship between the dis-trict and Talking Mountain is one of mutual tolerance rather than overt support or enthusiasm. As Ted describes it:

> They basically leave me alone. As far as other kinds of things like leadership roles within the building or whatever, there's no overt

attempt to restrict that from happening. It's more structural. There are not opportunities created for that to happen. There isn't time basically for it to happen. It's not sanctioned overtly. In faculty meetings, dialogue, exploration, struggle, investigation, the trading of strategies, the work of teachers exhibited or highlighted by the principal—as the kinds of things I'd really like to see going on in-side my school—is not part of the package so the atmosphere withers and dies. There's no encouragement for it. It's not that someone consciously set up rules, barriers, structures against it. It's just that there's no atmosphere to support it. It's like trying to grow wheat without water.

It is in this atmosphere that Ted works.

THE PERSON

Ted himself is a compelling study. He wears faded blue jeans, a belt with a Talking Mountain buckle, shoes that look to have walked a couple hundred miles to school and back. His sleeves are always rolled up; his fingers are long, artistic, tapping, pointing, moving. His voice is deep and resonant. His presence varies depending on the audience: He is quiet and thoughtful with adults, but more extro-verted, affectionate, and alive with students, who call him Newt. With potential funding sources, he is outright charming. With large crowds, he is charismatic, radiating a deep personal and intellectual passion that can move people to tears. He is a tall, thin, lanky man who gives a kind of physical definition to intensity. When he is angered or excited, a redness strengthens his face—what the students jokingly called "the suntanned glare of trouble." He moves a good deal—paces, kneels, stands, turns around, sits, and then moves again. He uses more of the space around him than other people. He spreads things out on the floor when working with students or slides onto his knees in order to get a better sighting on a student's problem. He uses his body in a way that suggests he is aware that, for many students, it is nearly impossible to sit still for long. His mind seems in constant motion as well, turning thoughts over and around, curious, rigorous, contemplative. Never, in any conversation I had with him or observed, did I hear him answer a complex question with a simple response. His responses built divergent cases or developed the complexity of a given circumstance rather than trying to simplify it. Most of his responses begin with, "It depends . . . ," or, "You can look at that from a couple of angles . . ."

He manages an enormous work load and an exhausting schedule. He works 10-hour days between the school and the office, and then works evenings correcting papers, writing for professional journals, creating his own curriculum guides, and corresponding with board members, fellow teachers, or policymakers. His recently published book chronicling his experiences was reviewed by all the major publications in the country and won two major book awards. He team-teaches two of his four classes in order to function as a mentor for other Talking Mountain staff members; through their teaming, the practice and the philosophy become clearer. On weekends, he makes himself available to students who need extra help by inviting them to drop by his home. In the winter months, he teaches one evening a week for two local universities. In the summer, he teaches several 1- or 2-week-long institutes for teachers at different universities around the country. While I observed, 18 visitors trooped through his classroom and met with him in the evening and during his planning period to discuss his projects. Furthermore, he serves on two dozen boards and advisory councils and gives speeches throughout the United States. Ted has a master's degree in teaching from a well-known university.

Although I was frequently exhausted by the demands on his time and energy, Ted seemed restrained only by the necessity to get a few hours of sleep. The fact that he is a single man with few family obligations obviously has allowed him to focus so much of his energy on his work. Ted is an example of a completely committed teacher. In his father's words, he is "damned enthusiastic!"

A TALKING MOUNTAIN DAY

The morning was fresh, clear, promising; as I drove up the mountainside to Ted's office, the dogwoods bloomed white, looking like young May Day girls running through the trees, practicing spring rituals. His office, an old log cabin, sits in the middle of the mountainside and breathes in quiet and tranquility—it is not the normal school or central office environment in which most teachers work but a quick step back 100 years. No sound of cars, no horns—only birds, creaking trees, buzzing insects. Just outside the cabin door is an old-fashioned garden surrounded by a split rail fence. Several kittens roll around in the catnip that is flourishing. The cabin is divided into two floors; the first houses tools, mountain artifacts, birdhouses, landscaping plans, a coffee pot. This floor is the office of the groundskeeper, himself a teacher and a self-professed student of hillbillyism.

The second story is divided into three rooms. Ted spends a couple of hours here every morning before going to the local public high school to teach four periods of English. Ted's office is a large room with counter space running the circumference of the room. Piles of books, light tables for photography work, stacks of cross-hatched papers ring the room. The room is covered in dust and the windows are framed once in wood and twice in spider webs—one senses that unless the piles are used frequently, they will disintegrate into gray. There are several stools, a large table in the center of the room on which sit more piles of paper—these more active, dust free—what appears to be an ancient typewriter, a few ashtrays, and a coffee cup or two. The walls are rough-hewn, plain and simple. There is nothing on the walls except a few past covers of the magazine and a poster from a TV special with which the Talking Mountain staff and students were involved.

Ted is perched on a stool, working with two other staff members who manage the day-to-day operations of their nonprofit corporation. Kate, who handles the foundation work of the organization, has been with the corporation for 10 years and is the heart of the office. Maggie is the business manager and keeps track of all the budgets. Everyone is dressed in jeans and cowboy boots or other shoes appropriate to the muddy, unpaved mountain road that leads up onto the property. The morning's work is focused on administrative details. They review budgets, analyze the last two months' spending, discuss reporting procedures to the several foundations that have made substantial grants to support their work. Ted and Kate go over his schedule for the next 2 weeks, and he gives her a list of people he needs to meet with on his Wednesday trip into the nearby metropolitan area where he instructs an evening course for teachers on curriculum design. The contacts they are arranging are with potential board members and a few foundation people who might be interested in supporting their work. The emphasis is on purposeful utilization of time; he does not want to spend any more time in the city than absolutely necessary. He reminds Kate to contact the governor's office to make sure that the citation of exemplary service comes in time for one of their staff members who is leaving. He paces in an attempt to shake loose any forgotten details, and questions Shirley, another secretary, about the paper trail they are maintaining on one of their projects. He tells her what to file and where. As the meeting concludes, Kate hands him a large package—a gift from the teacher outreach coordinator for their network in a neighboring southern state. He unfolds a large, shocking pink velvet painting of Elvis. He chuckles and tacks it up on the wall. Several other employees wander in to investigate. Although he clearly thinks it's a joke, several others look troubled—is it a joke or not?

Ted jumps in his truck and roars off to school, which is about 10 miles away. It is a new county high school with a beautiful, fenced campus just outside the small town of Wilmer. A guard sits at the gate and waves Newt in. The school sits on a hill surrounded by low, rolling mountains, blue and hazy in the spring warmth. Approximately 840 students attend the school, grades 7 through 12. Ted is the senior staff member there.

His second-period class is advanced journalism where the students generate a magazine four times a year. He walks into the class, already in progress, which he team-teaches with another teacher who works for Talking Mountain. Four students are sprawled on the floor looking at a layout, several photos, and some typed text. Several others are transcribing taped recordings of interviews with people from the local community, hunched over a tape recording, comparing their transcriptions, line by line. Others are visiting. Some are in the plywood darkroom that protrudes into the room; two more sit at old computer stations in a corner. Betty, the co-teacher, works with those students on the computers. Ted stops by each group, says hello, and checks the students' progress. The atmosphere is relaxed yet businesslike; the students are confident and engaged, and do not stop what they are doing unless they have a question for him. Ted introduces me, but visitors are commonplace, so my presence creates no disturbance.

The room itself is an interesting study; it bears slim resemblance to the hundreds of classrooms I have visited. There are mountain-culture artifacts in the entryway, stacked on top of filing cabinets and shelving—quilts, jugs, butter churns, whirligigs, old chairs, wood carvings, old plow pieces, a poster: "If you think education is expensive, try ignorance." There is a large map of the United States that is being eaten by stacks of paper growing from the counter up. The map has pins stuck in it to keep track of the places Ted and his students have visited during the year to give speeches about what they are doing. The pins go from one side of the country to the other. There are large filing cabinets that hold student files, layouts, photography equipment, rulers, yardsticks, glue, and tape recorders. Another large cabinet holds books that resulted from the magazines, stacks of past copies of the magazines, Ted's personal files. His desk is buried in paper—piles on the floor, the chair, on the open drawers. One blackboard—or rather a modern white board—has the publication deadline for the next edition of the magazine. It lists whose articles will go where, how many pages, the title. Student desks are arranged into a "U" shape around the middle of the room. Ted circles the room, and checks the piles to make sure that everything is in order. There are no sets of textbooks anywhere in sight, but several shelves contain reference books. The state guidelines are written on large poster board on the wall. On the north counter, I count 10 trophies and awards—Teacher of the Year, a citation from the House of Representatives, awards for writing, for teaching, for student achievement—all shoved there in forgotten disarray. I ask about which of the awards mean the most to him:

> Depends on who from and what for. The book I wrote for teachers won two awards. The star teacher awards—I like those—has to do with student awards—highest SAT scores. The student is picked in February and then picks a teacher who has made a difference for them. Those have been real nice. As far as the rest of them go, they don't mean much to me. They usually don't come out of a personal appreciation of what really is going on. The only ones I really care about are the awards given for a product.

Ted and Betty range from student group to student group during the course of the class period, checking progress, offering suggestions, sitting down to help solve problems. At 10:25, Betty yells, "It's nearly 10:30, y'all. Put your stuff where nobody else can get at it." At 10:30 students begin to move in and out. Ted stands ready to greet those leaving and arriving. A blond student named Mark comes in, calling out for Ted, lugging the SAT guide, and looking terrifically worried—his eyes as wide as they can go. He sits down in a desk and thrusts the book at Ted. "D'you see this? I gotta get 400 in MATH to get into college. You see the MATH? It's stuff I've never seen before. I can't do it. I'll never make it." The words come out in a desperate rush, and then stop short, in defeat. Ted drops to his knees in front of Mark and centers him squarely in his line of vision. "Hold up now, slow down. Let's look at this. When do you have to take this?"

"Next spring."

"Okay. So, we spend an hour a week working over the stuff. I'll do it with you. Did you talk to the math teacher? She'll help, too."

"She hates me. I'm always cutting up in there. I told her about it already. She said I have a long way to go."

"Whoa now. I want you to think about this." Ted speaks slowly:

> Every teacher in this school took that test and made it through. Think of all the students in your classes who are going off to college this year. They all made it through. This test is not too tough for you. I have another copy of one of the prep books. It's on my desk. You set up the time and I'll work with you. First we'll do your book, then we'll do mine. You can do it, okay? And you better stop cutting up in math class if you want to get any help in there, all right?

Mark's eyes relax. He grins, his body relaxes for a moment, and he says, "Okay. Thanks. If all my teachers were like you . . ." He bolts down the hall, book in hand.

Mark later explained to me that he had only just recently decided to go to college:

> I failed seventh grade—didn't try, liked girls and all that. I felt like school was a waste of time. When I got to ninth grade, I didn't like my first English teacher—she was giving me trouble. We come in and did a composition on summer. Then we went over nouns and pronouns which we have went over since I was in fourth grade.

The basics. I didn't like it; I've done it all the way through elementary school. I was bored. If you tried to tell her something that might be more interesting, she'd pitch a fit and write you up. My cousin Jake got me in here. [The two boys wanted to write a story about their grandfather who had been reading the Talking Mountain magazines since they first were published.] I wrote one composition and Newt took me with him to make a speech. Newt thought I did all right so he scheduled another one in a school. We talked in front of principals and teachers. Everybody thought I done all right and so I went with him to New York. I made a speech there to about 400 people. Me and Newt got a standing ovation. Then we went to a play, ice skating, all over the city. . . . Then me and Jake went with him to the University of Georgia where we saw some guys from here who used to be our heroes— you know, football players. We went to classes with them and then made our speech and from there I decided to go to college. My cousin Jake was trying to figure out where to go; I just figured out I wanted to go!

Back in the classroom, it becomes apparent that the time in between classes is very important to Ted. He uses it to connect with students, to check on their lives in general, to express his great affection for them. He moves around the room and hugs a few of the students—big, lunky boys who don't cringe but turn with genuine affection to say hello, to punch him on the arm. I have never seen this kind of affectionate exchange before between male students and a male teacher. Two students—a boy and a girl—walk in with matching black T-shirts with the boy's car airbrushed in metallic colors on the front. Everyone oohs and aaahs. Ted grins and asks them where they had the masterpiece done. The other students are interested too. They describe a booth at the county fairgrounds. The room fills up to overflowing. Two other teachers who work for Talking Mountain come in. The students in this class are younger, more rambunctious. This is the beginning Talking Mountain course where they learn the skills of magazine production, radio production, video production, musical performance. Eventually, the students swirl into an orderly, expectant quiet. Ted reviews the agenda for the week. He gets a progress report from each of the groups of students who are working together on a project. Progress report completed, he reminds them that they have visitors coming from several other states, so they need to reassemble for the last 15 minutes of the class period to answer questions.

Everyone disperses in different directions and it sounds a lot like the breakup of the cops' meetings on the television show "Hill Street Blues." Some go to the music rooms with Frank, who teaches music, songwriting, and music recording. Several disappear with Tom, who teaches video and radio production. There is much jostling, tossing of jackets and folders, shouted arrangements to meet later. Those who remain settle into working groups spread around the room. Ted moves toward Larry, a tall blond student who has a crew cut and wears dark sunglasses; he looks to be a senior. Ted hands Larry a song Larry has written. Ted has typed the song for Larry and corrected the spelling problems. Larry looks it over and seems surprised. Ted tells him that it is really coming along and that Larry now needs to work on the piece that explains how he wrote it. Ted asks him to put the successive drafts of the piece in order so that he, Ted, can look at them. Larry nods and spends the rest of the period working by himself. He writes some and sits some. Under his breath, Ted wonders whether the student is accomplishing anything today.

Ted notes that Larry was nearly a lost cause, in and out of school, hardly able to read or write. Each day was a struggle for him to participate until he wrote a song, set it to music, and sang it to the class. It was a good song and the students were really proud of him. Ted and the other teachers typed up his work every night so that he could see it without misspellings and the other collected problems. Gradually, he has become more confident, more interested, more productive. I ask Ted if it bothers him that his room becomes a dumping ground for problem students. "No, but they send them so late. How can I make a difference in the face of a lifetime of defeat?" Larry should be a senior chronologically but holds sophomore standing.

Toward the end of the class period, the students reassemble to answer the questions of the seven teachers who have come to visit from two neighboring states. The teachers have come to spend 2 days observing in Talking Mountain classrooms and meeting with Ted and the rest of the staff about their own work. These are teachers who took a 2-week curriculum course from Ted during the previous summer and are currently involved in experiential education projects of their own creation with their students. The visitors ask about the nature of the students' working together—how close they all seem. They ask whether it is the work itself that inspires that kind of community. Suzie, a ninth-grade student who has just completed the first draft of a major video project, describes their relationship. "Here's how Newt looks at it. He's married to Talking Mountain. Talking Mountain is his wife and we're all his kids and Frank and Tom and Betty—they're his in-laws!" Ted grins, looks a little sheepish, and turns red. Everyone roars with laughter while the students go on to say that they work harder in these conditions than they do in regular classrooms, putting in extra hours—coming early and leaving late. They claim that the work is just plain more interesting. Soon the students and visitors leave—the students to go to other classes, the visitors to go to the guesthouse at Talking Mountain. On their way out the door, Kara, a young girl with hair moussed into spikes of pure punk, announces that her mother is using a picture of her father for a dartboard lately. They were divorced a year ago. It is a harsh comment, and her friends respond with uncomfortable silence.

The fourth-period class comes in. These students are working on research as part of their college-bound English curriculum. Ted kneels on the floor in the center of the group as they brainstorm how Jeffrey will interview a local Native American—a Cherokee—about the customs of his tribe. Jeff arranged the interview, which they expect to take place sometime during the next week. While one of the students records information on the board, the others generate, then categorize, then prioritize. Ted speaks only to focus the group. A secretary blasts in over the intercom, "Newt, do you have Nancy Little in your room this period?"

"Yep, she's here, but she's down in the business ed. room."

"Could you please send her down here when she gets back? I need to clear up her records."

"Yes, ma'am." And the class resumes, interrupted both when Nancy comes in and when she returns. By the time the class leaves, they have organized Jeff's interview in such a way that he will be able to gather information that is then already partially organized for his research paper. In addition, the other students have discussed how they can use the same process to order their interviews. Ted encourages them to work with other students when they do their interview preparation because, clearly, many heads are better than one.

Lunchtime. Students and teachers swarm to the lunchroom—a

large cafeteria. The noise is worse than an airport; everyone is talking at once. The teachers sit at a central table and eat fast. They talk between bites. One staff member tells me that she'd love to know what goes on in Ted's room, but that she's never been there. Ted invites her in—anytime. Several of us get into a hot discussion of the national writing project. Ted has very strong feelings about it— that it has not gone far enough, that it leaves teachers unprepared to translate the experience into real curriculum for students. Bill, another Talking Mountain staff member, says, "It's like pushing them out on the freeway with no gas." Another teacher is discussing a parent who assaulted her recently. She is clearly outraged. Someone else asks Ted about something in his book. He answers quickly and races off to smoke a quick cigarette before returning to class. Thirty minutes does not go very far.

Fifth period is college prep English—a large, rambunctious class. One student announces that he has gotten a job working at the local airport as a result of a research project he did on how a small local airport is managed and funded. He wants to fly more than anything, and they all cheer. Eventually, they settle into a kind of noisy cooperation. They have a discussion about what constitutes a good definition paper. Ted offers them several examples that he has pulled from contemporary writers—all different in form and approach. They analyze each and then discuss possibilities of their own. He outlines the expectations for this assignment—when it is due, when he will look at drafts, what kind of thing he will be looking for, how this particular assignment matches the state guidelines the students need to meet before graduation. The students are invited to challenge the deadlines and to question the evaluation procedures, which they do, but in a conscientious and responsible manner. There is no whining or complaining but rather a clarification, a mutual sense-making. He comments to me that the group is rowdy and that he holds them with a tenuous if powerful thread—graduation credit. He roams the room, sliding onto his knees for better proximity with students, sitting down at the worktables, disappearing into the darkroom. The students work in various ways. Some sit in groups and talk about what they might write about. Others work in twos. Several look through a couple of the examples. Several other students work alone, beginning to write already. Two girls near me decide that maybe they will define a "kegger." Everyone laughs and they proceed to toss out details. Ted does not censor their topics, nor does he moderate the conversations, but moves around to answer questions, to participate in their thinking-through.

Sixth period is Ted's planning period. As the students stream in and out of his classroom, he tries to pull the things he needs to do together. He stacks papers that need looking at, makes notes to himself, talks to students, checks with Betty, and rearranges the piles of papers. In a relatively short period of time, most of the students disappear except for a few who have been excused from their other classrooms to work on their projects for Ted. Mark comes in to work on his layout. Another girl sits down at a computer to work on her article. Ted congregates with Frank and Tom—his co-teachers—so that they can go over the class they are teaching together. He spreads everything out on a back table. Another teacher arrives dressed formally in a suit. Ted sits down with him, having forgotten that the fellow asked to meet today. The visitor asks for advice on how to become more entrepreneurial in teaching. Ted briefly shares how he orchestrated his circumstances and asks questions about the visitor's interests. The visitor leaves after another 20 minutes. Ted shrugs—not sure that he has been of any help, unclear as to what the guy wanted from him. Ted checks what Mark is doing, pats him on the back, and sits down with Tom and Frank. They discuss coming deadlines, where the students are, and how they might expedite completion of these projects. They run through the list of their students to make sure that each of them is getting the support needed to feel successful. In the process, they each take responsibility for following up with several students. They talk about the curriculum guides that Frank and Tom are writing on video production and music making. Neither is very far along and both look a bit ashamed. Ted reinforces coming deadlines and suggests ways to protect writing time.

The special education teacher comes in for a bit of advice on the magazine her students are doing, inspired by Ted's students. They joke and swap quips when a faculty meeting is called over the intercom. Everyone groans. There is never a warning, never time to conjure up an excuse. The bell rings to signal the end of the day. As students stream out of the school, Mark's mother and his cousin, Jake, come in to finish their layout. The mom sits down at the computer, while the staff moves toward the library and the faculty meeting.

The faculty meeting is held in the library. The room fills slowly, and teachers cluster at tables with their friends. Talk ranges across the day's activities. The meeting is called together by a counselor and consists of a series of announcements. "The district is short on testing booklets and number 2 pencils. Please don't lose the testing booklet and remember to collect the pencils." The principal, a large man in his mid-40s, stands up to take over. He speaks with a deep southern drawl:

> Make sure you folks are teaching 50 minutes of the period every day. I know that spring is a more relaxed time and that it's hard to keep the kids working. Still, it's hard for us to justify our work if we're doing nothing. I don't want to see you giving busy work, either. We should be pushing the kids right up to the end. I have little free time myself to be dealing with problems and complaints from parents and kids. The busier they are, the less time I have to spend dealing with messes.

Without any discussion, he moves on to the copyright law and the problems they are having with illegal videotapes. He calls on Ms. Beth to explain the law and asks that the teachers erase those tapes that are illegal. He then asks a series of questions at random, "Mr. Long, how do you use standardized test scores in your classroom?"

Mr. Long hemmed, hawed, and then responded, "Well, I look at the test scores when I see a student in jeopardy, when it looks like he or she might not make it. Pretty much, I rely on the counselors to use the test scores when placing students."

Without comment, the principal singles out the home economics teacher. "Rinnie, how do you meet the state guidelines in your classroom?"

She pauses, turns red, then answers, "Well, the state guidelines require that the kids know a lot about nutrition, so during the year we cover the four food groups, and we talk about how important proper nutrition is to general health . . . is that what you want to know?"

The principal says it is and that he is not asking the questions for sport but because the state monitors could show up at any time, and he wants the staff to be able to answer their questions with some semblance of intelligence. He dismisses the staff with a promise of more questions like these asked at random. As we leave the faculty meeting, I ask whether the principal always uses such a positive approach with the staff—accusing them of slacking off in the spring and then giving pop quizzes. Tom, walking with Ted and me, is quick to respond, "He's one helluva lot better than the last one."

The Talking Mountain staff moves back into Ted's classroom for a meeting of their own that is regularly scheduled every Tuesday afternoon. The staff from the offices up on the mountain drift in. Several students work in the background on their projects. There is a warm exchange between the Talking Mountain staff and the students—everyone is addressed on a first-name basis. Bill writes agenda items on the chalkboard. As others come in, they add more items:

Student summer jobs
Debrief Davidson meeting
New board members
Visit requests
Budget
Fellows program
Doubleday request
Photos for Cleveland

The group pulls chairs into a circle. Ted is visiting privately with another teacher who comes in dressed in a suit. The new visitor is applying for the department chairship for the school and wants to visit with Ted to find out about his program. As he leaves, the meeting convenes, called to order by Bill. One of the secretaries asks the group to prioritize the agenda. That done, they ask the students working the room to leave for a few minutes while they launch into a thoughtful discussion about the students who need and have applied for student summer work. The grants and royalties from their projects allow the Talking Mountain staff to hire both students and community members during the summer to continue the regular course work, to work on the land, and to archive the collections of artifacts they have accumulated. They discuss quietly who would benefit the most from which job: "I think that young Mike is close to making a decision about whether to go the voc[ational] or college track. If we give him the right jolt, he might head down the more interesting track . . ." The conversation is different because, rather than competing for excellent students, the staff seems most concerned about how to support individual students to foster their growth and skills. Comments about students were couched in positive terms. During the entire time I was in Wilmer, I did not hear any negative student talk. "If I was to pick the prettiest egg for my basket, I'd choose Cynthia, and leave the rest to lay . . ." And so the discussion proceeds, never devaluing a student but working to find the right jobs for the students, ones that will extend their skills, build their confidence, allow them to complete projects they did not have the time to do during the regular class period, during the school year. That discussion completed, the students are invited to come back in, and several of them work through the entire meeting.

As the group runs through the agenda items, Ted accumulates a list of decisions he will bring to the attention of the Talking Mountain students in the magazine classes. The decisions affect the activities of the Talking Mountain classes and in some cases have significant budget implications. These decisions are presented to the students for their voting approval. Do they want to host a group of Russian students for a couple of weeks in the winter? Do they want to release some of the Talking Mountain photographs for use by other students in Cleveland? Do they want to work with a storyteller who wishes to turn some of the students' articles into oral stories? Do they want to interview the two candidates for the intern program for next year? All the staff seem very comfortable with the notion that the students will, in many ways, determine faculty work load for the coming months, depending on what they choose to become involved in.

Ted describes the results of several meetings with potential donors, while they discuss the $200,000 deficit they will shortly face. The meeting goes until after 7 p.m.

The staff thoughtfully and carefully went through each agenda item. There were no breaks, though people got up and walked around a bit and several people stood just outside the door and smoked, using an ashtray that Ted materialized from somewhere. At the end of the meeting, they reviewed who needed to do what before their next meeting. On his way out the door, Ted handed me half of his college English papers that needed grading. He himself faced a quick evening meeting with the visitors who were staying in the Talking Mountain guesthouse, some urgent paper-grading, some correspondence, and, finally, planning for his university class to be taught the next evening. This was certainly not the 8 a.m. to 3 p.m. day that most teaching contracts describe.

The evening meeting in the guesthouse was informal and full of fun. The group of teachers from two states shared a strong rapport because they had taken Ted's 2-week-long course during the summer. There was an air of festivity. The invitation to come to Talking Mountain provided them with a rare opportunity to observe another teacher in action, to get out of their own districts, and to visit together. The group included their outreach network coordinator, Martha, who had obtained funding locally with the emotional support of the Talking Mountain staff to open an office for the specific purpose of providing a support system for those teachers who had taken Ted's course and wished to experiment with experiential education. Martha, the donor of the Elvis tapestry, was herself an expert in folk culture and, as a result, very helpful to the teachers. She organized meetings, visited their classrooms, kept them abreast of Talking Mountain projects, and encouraged them to write up their own experiences. While Martha fixed Ted a plate of her best southern biscuits, the other teachers briefly reported the status of their own projects. One teacher, Frank, and his ninth-grade students had just completed a recording of local southern musicians. The group of teachers described Frank as someone who was just about to give up on teaching after 15 years when he got excited about Ted's methods. The students had auditioned groups for the recording, hired a recording studio, obtained a loan from the bank to pay for the initial cut, and designed and wrote the brochure that accompanied the tape. In his conversation, Frank vacillated between great enthusiasm for this method of teaching and a kind of exhausted despair that he did not share with Ted, but did with me. He felt wrung out by the experience of trying to take care of all of the details associated with this project. Although the students were wildly motivated, they also took more of his time and energy. He was struggling, trying to figure out whether it is humanly possible to teach in this manner all the time and whether he could do it for more than one class a day.

Marlene, a second-grade teacher in an extremely conservative rural school district, was experimenting with methodology for second graders. Her students had done math projects, Jack Tale puppet shows to demonstrate math concepts, and various other activities. Although she was enthusiastic, her district administrators were not supportive of her innovations and were attempting to coerce her into moving to sixth grade for the next school year. After 30 years of service, she felt that she was being punished for working long and hard, and that her new experiments in better instruction were of little interest to the administrators.

Another woman, Margie, had been teaching for 22 years. Margie describes herself as, "Never was much of one for textbooks!" She and her sixth-grade students were researching the history of three old buildings in their community—the depot, the hotel, and the jail. Although none of the buildings was now used for its original purpose, her students had managed to trace their history from 1850 on. They were currently investigating the land usage prior to 1850. In the process, the students had become regulars at the city hall's archival records department and had become adept at using those resources. Margie's students wrote a magazine to record their findings.

Dolly, a staff member who works with the teacher networks, explained that these people were in the midst of a process. Most of them had just completed their first successful project, and so they were feeling pretty good. She anticipated more to come, which explained Frank's vacillating euphoria and depression:

> They seem to go in a cycle. First, they experiment. Then, they have a little success and they're jubilant. Then they get exhausted. Next they get militant, true believers. Nobody can talk to them, they alienate their friends. Then they move into settled practice. Sure, the process is slightly different for each of them, but they all seem to follow the pattern.

Ted listened to the project updates, offered a few suggestions, some encouragement, and then worked with the group to organize their schedule of observations for the next day. Each of them had particular interests, which Ted used to match with the Talking Mountain staff's teaching schedule. As Ted left, Martha followed him out the door, to get some advice on the running of the outreach network.

OTHER RESPONSIBILITIES

Although the day recounted here was fairly typical for Ted—
long, complex, demanding, ever changing—other days involved a
variety of activities all directed toward supporting Talking Mountain
so that they could continue to provide the kind of experiential
education for students that the staff believed so important. Other
days revolved around spreading the word about their work to other
teachers. On several occasions during my observations, we headed to
the city after fifth period to combine meetings with potential board
members or possible funders with the 4-hour class offered once a
week for teachers. On these days Ted donned a tie left permanently
for such occasions ·in the recesses of his car, which housed more
heaps of stuff, including boxes of examples of student work from
classrooms around the country, books, and music.

On one such occasion, Ted met with and described his work to
the head of one of the South's largest foundations. The older gentle-
man was so taken with Ted's work that he was inspired to tell of his
own greatest civic contribution, which had been to organize funds
that were used by their city to dispel the destructive race riots that
erupted elsewhere in the country following Martin Luther King's
assassination. The rapport between the two was remarkable in that
both of them were quite passionate about the need to make the world
a better place.

After this meeting, Ted raced out to the local (a 2-hour drive)
university campus to teach his course on curriculum change with Bill.
Again, the Talking Mountain staff had an exchange relationship with
the university that provided space and access to students while the
grants Talking Mountain had secured paid salaries and expenses of
running a course away from home. Because Ted did not have a
doctorate, Bill was the official instructor of record.

When we walked into the classroom, 25 teachers were waiting.
Ted and Bill ran the class much as they did their classrooms with
high school students. They posted the evening's agenda and then
asked the teachers to make revisions. Several of the teachers suggested that they would like to have the opportunity for the group to
help them troubleshoot the projects they were doing with their own
students. Ted rearranged the agenda, leaving time for a visit from

several teachers who had taken the class the previous year. Those teachers were bringing some of their students to talk about their own curriculum projects and the procedures involved. The class moved from a discussion of Dewey's work, which they were all reading, to a discussion of their own projects. One large black woman was bursting with excitement. She taught fifth graders who had decided that they wanted to improve the billboards in the city. The woman had had no idea of how to help them do that and had tried to discourage them, but because the students were insistent, she made a few phone calls. After a couple of hours on the phone one afternoon, she had obtained the right to have her class work on two billboards sponsored by a company that wanted to work with the schools. She caught her students' enthusiasm and was very excited about the project, but still didn't know what to do next. She wanted help from the rest of the group to try to figure that out. In just the same way Ted had shown his fourth-period class how to organize an interview, he showed this group of teachers how to begin a project, how to share the decision making with their students, how to ensure rigor in the project, and how to meet the state guidelines without following the withering curriculum guides.

At this point, visitors from the course Ted had conducted at this university the previous year arrived to share their experiences. The group then listened to three teachers and their students summarize their projects. One group had done a newspaper of current world events written for students at the middle school level. Another woman, a librarian, had recorded several oral histories for the library. After the sharing, the visitors left and Ted and Bill encouraged the class participants to discuss how they felt about teaching in the way they were suggesting. What followed was a very frank discussion. Some of the teachers just did not believe that they had the energy to do this in addition to their already overloaded schedules. Several others were very excited and well under way. One, who was in his second year of teaching and was having significant difficulty managing his students, was afraid to try the new techniques because he believed that he would lose the little control he currently had. Ted was sympathetic to the young man's plight as he himself had felt the same way as a young teacher. He communicated to the beginner that experience had led him to the belief that a more participatory curriculum really helped with classroom management, even though it might seem to lead to potentially greater chaos. Ted and Bill facilitated a discussion rather than attempting to answer all the concerns. Their stated hope was that during the run of the course many of the concerns would be answered. On these days, Ted arrived home at 11 p.m., with no dinner and with stacks of papers demanding attention.

Once during my observations, he loaded his car with several students and headed off to the next state to make a speech for a group of teachers interested in changing their curriculum. Such speeches were common in his schedule. During the 3-month period prior to my observations, Ted made 17 speeches in 11 different cities in 8 states. Most of those speeches were delivered to teacher groups and were focused on the Talking Mountain experience, the teaching philosophy, and the importance of providing a meaningful educational experience for students. Most frequently, he took students with him to provide them with additional educational opportunities, believing that when students had to explain what it was that they had learned in his courses, it deepened their understanding.

In a recent speech delivered in a western state, Ted brought two of his students with him. He spoke of the need for teachers to take greater leadership responsibility for changing the curriculum so that it provided more meaningful experiences for students. After describing his own philosophy, and the Talking Mountain projects, he had the two students describe their own experiences in his classes. The first student described a research project he had done to dispel the stereotypes of mountain hillbillies. Delivered in a southern mountain drawl, the talk delineated how folks think that most people who talk like him are dumb, stupid, and drink moonshine. He then described what he had found out about hillbillies—that they were strong people who took care of themselves in the face of great adversity. He concluded by describing how much he had learned and why it was important to him. His previous experiences in school, much like the one Mark described when I was observing at Talking Mountain, left him bored and uninterested in working hard. He thanked the teachers in attendance for listening to him and for caring enough about students to try to make schools better places.

The second student, a senior hoping to get into the Air Force Academy, described his experience. By the time he was a senior, he had published over 100 pages of text in a magazine, had helped to work on a television script, had done Smithsonian quality archiving, and had worked over the period of a semester on a research project during which he interviewed primary sources, reviewed secondary sources, and shaped those data into a meaningful picture. He felt that he had had a top-quality school experience and knew how to push himself to do his best. By the time the students were finished, no one at my table, including the men, had dry eyes. On the way out, several teachers mentioned that Ted had provoked them to carefully reconsider their own curriculum and instructional techniques.

HIS COLLEAGUES

While at Talking Mountain, I had formal conversations with four teachers, and many others informally. Some of the informal conversations were with teachers who were taking Ted's course at the metropolitan university. Others were teachers who came to visit Ted's classroom and who had participated in the summer courses taught at other universities in other states. In addition, Ted shared with me some of the correspondence from other teachers, which he received on a daily basis. Ted's circumstances were unique in that he did not hold any formal leadership position in his school and, therefore, was not expected to influence his colleagues in any way. Still, many of them had taken his course and had worked with him for a number of years. I was interested to know how they felt about his work and whether it influenced theirs in any way. I interviewed only teachers who had taken his course.

The formal interviews were conducted with teachers whom Ted characterized as (1) a strong supporter, (2) an indifferent colleague, (3) the local Association representative, and (4) a nonsupporter. All were more than willing to participate and gave up their planning time in order to visit with me. None of them were aware of Ted's perceptions of their reaction to his work. These teachers defined teacher leadership in terms of the traditional roles with which they were familiar—union representatives, department heads, and committee chairs. None of them found it easy to conceptualize other kinds of leadership roles for teachers, mainly because they had not thought about it before. Within the group there was a consensus that Ted provided enormous leadership for the other teachers in the building, even though he did not hold any of the formal positions they had mentioned. One participant noted, "He [Ted] has created his leadership role by having the courage to change the ordinary format of education."

He provided leadership for them in a variety of ways. Although many of them had never seen him teach the students, they had taken a course he offered for their staff earlier in the year. Several of them noted that it was the best college course they had ever had because it was informal, participatory, and had valued their experience as teachers. "His course was much better than my other college classes. It was the first time I sat through four hours and was not bored to tears. I really felt I could use the stuff." At the same time, Ted communicated a strong philosophy of what public education should be like for students, and challenged the group to examine their teaching practices and principles.

> He's taught me to stand back and to look at the whole picture. He and Bill [the staff member who team-teaches the Talking Mountain courses for teachers with Ted] have been true leaders for me. They encouraged me to believe what I've always known was true. He's helped me to justify what I knew I should be doing. I never had any of this stuff in any of my ed. classes. He's really taught me a whole new way of thinking, a new way of approaching problems—how to look at problems, to be more analytical.

In addition, they believed that he provided leadership by sharing what he gleaned in his travels around the country. They did not perceive him as a quasi-administrator, because the work he did was clearly focused on instruction and work with students. They also valued the hundreds of outside educators who came throughout the school year to visit his classroom. The visitors gave them a kind of exposure to the larger educational community they would never have had otherwise. Furthermore, the teachers were well aware of the fact that he provided excellent public relations for them. They noted that he was very well respected by the students and had very high expectations for them, plus he was loved by the community. One teacher claimed that "his reputation prevents the administration from touching him."

Responses from other teachers in the informal conversations

were similar and revolved around the contribution he had made in both curriculum development and instruction. A special education teacher told me about the enormous effect his class had had on her students. She had showed her small group of severely and profoundly handicapped students a copy of the magazine developed by Ted's students. One of the boys, named John, reared his head back and said, "I reckon we can do that!" The inspiration Ted's students' work had provided carried her students forward into a magazine of their own. The project led her students, who are so often unchallenged and ignored, to work collaboratively, to deal with community members, and to produce a product of which they were all very proud. Many accounts of the effects of his leadership came from those people who had taken his course and corresponded with him. For example:

> I think the thing that I realized at [the course] was that this philosophy of yours could accomplish everything I wanted to see happen in a different way. I knew it would work because of the way you had made me feel during the workshop. The students read from their writings on Wednesday at the lodge and parents were there who were very literate but there were also parents there who couldn't read. And it seemed to me that we brought both of those together—families with rare items took pride in those and did not feel badly and also saw that what their children were doing with words was also important. That involves complex dynamics. . . . I have tried to tell you this in other letters. Maybe I have been successful. I don't know. But where I am with this process of yours is at such a wonderful point. I see more every day. I understand and respect the complexity of the process you have introduced me to. It is almost as if I have been led into some mysterious place where discoveries are made each day. I continue to fail but I do not feel badly because I know in time, I can do better. I am on the right track. . . . That's what it is all about, isn't it?

To summarize, Ted's colleagues at his own school perceived him to be a strong leader by virtue of the example he set. His own perceptions of their reactions to his work were not accurate, because, indeed, they were all very enthusiastic about his efforts. Despite their enthusiasm, however, he noted that the Talking Mountain staff and a couple of other teachers used the methods he described, but that he did not believe that very many others were interested in trying them out nor in finding out more about them. He found this pretty discouraging.

CHARACTERISTICS OF TALKING MOUNTAIN TEACHER LEADERSHIP

As I tried to understand Ted's role, I began to look for identifying characteristics—some characteristics that could be examined in each of the three stories. They are:

1. the purpose of the role
2. the incentives undergirding the role
3. the assumptions the role makes about teachers, students, learning, and leading
4. the effects the role has on students
5. the challenges the role poses to the school
6. the kinds of collaborative relationships the role established

To begin, Ted's case was different from that of the other two. His position was never established to influence people in his own building; that was not part of his original thinking as he began to start teacher outreach centers. Still, he talked frequently about how discouraging it was for him to have found so much success and to be such an isolated pocket in his school. Two years prior to my arrival, he had taught his course for teachers in the area and several from his own building had come. It is important, however, to understand that the original intention of the position was not to influence practice in his own building.

Ted and the Talking Mountain staff never talked about teacher leadership or the kind of leadership roles they were trying to create; they were too busy trying to understand the network they'd created and to communicate with its members. When I thought about Ted's role, it became clear that he modeled the kind of leadership he was trying to promote in other teachers through the teacher outreach network. In a variety of ways, his concept of teacher leadership might be called "teachers leading teachers." His courses are set up so that he and other Talking Mountain staff teach courses for teachers to encourage experimentation with experience based methodology.

Once teachers have taken the course, and have experimented in their own classrooms, they are invited to join a larger network of teachers who are using similar methods. The Talking Mountain staff avoid the "one best way" syndrome, and encourage teachers to try their own approaches and share them with others by describing the pedagogy as a continual, progressive development rather than a cookbook of activities. Teachers are encouraged to experiment with various forms and in a variety of disciplines.

This form of teacher leadership is undergirded by a set of implicit assumptions that communicate a good deal about teachers and teaching.

1. Powerful learning is experience-based and relates to real life. Traditional teaching in schools does not foster these kinds of learning experiences.
2. Students are fully capable of demonstrating what they are learning.
3. Teachers need the opportunity to experiment with these methods.
4. The philosophy of experiential education is ages old. Examples abound both in history and in current practice.
5. Teachers learn more about changing their practice when they learn from other teachers.
6. Teachers need the opportunity to work together with other teachers when they are experimenting because it reduces the discomfort and the uncertainty and increases the pool of solutions to problems.
7. Teachers and students collaboratively develop curriculum.

Although these assumptions are not set down explicitly in a list like this, they are nevertheless understood and shared. Many of the teachers I visited with described Ted's class and their collaboration with others as the most powerful learning experiences they had ever had because the courses were taught by teachers, because they were generating their own curriculum, and because their students were involved in really producing something of use to the community—magazines, videotapes, brochures on safety or environmental issues, to mention just a few.

Teacher leadership as the Talking Mountain staff encouraged it did not require systematic changes. Teachers worked in their individual classrooms and traveled to nearby universities in the evenings or during the summer in order to take the courses. The gatherings of network teachers were organized during their free time. In order to visit other classrooms, teachers took personal leave days or asked for a substitute. Although the master schedule, the salary schedule, and the length of the class period were not challenged, teachers were required to give of their own time in order to participate.

Teachers' incentives to participate arise out of their personal commitment to provide the very best educational experience for kids. A second set of incentives arise out of heightened student motivation and out of the tangible results of teachers' and students' work found in the products the projects produced.

Teacher leadership in Ted's case involve two types of collegiality. Ted spent most of his time mentoring other teachers. He had used the methodology for such a long time that it was second nature to him. Still he persisted in trying to communicate it to others. He also offered the opportunity for participating teachers to collaborate and to take on leadership if they felt so inclined. Implicit in the invitation to participate was a kind of leadership density model suggesting that there is room for a multitude of leaders. The term "leadership density" comes from Meyer's (1971) work in which he suggests that systems that provide only a few leadership positions are too restrictive and do not foster the growth and development of the wealth of human resources that exist in any given staff. He describes a system of leadership density where numbers of people within a given organization have the opportunity to contribute in meaningful ways. Ted communicates that each teacher who chooses to participate can lead others to a clearer understanding of the possibilities in this kind of instruction.

DOMINANT THEMES

Several dominant themes emerge from examining Ted Newton's story. In the midst of a traditional system, not geared in any way to support teacher innovation, one teacher flourished to provide fine educational experiences for the students with whom he worked and leadership for teachers around the country. How had this happened? With the development of teacher outreach centers, what information were they uncovering about how to improve the quality of instruction in classrooms, and how to change traditional teacher behaviors? The themes were both provocative and revealing.

Valuing Students

Ted and his colleagues met frequently and worked constantly with students. During the course of my visit in the school, I never heard any of the staff members disparage a student in any way. There was none of the sarcastic banter about problem students that I hear so frequently in schools. No one blamed students for their ineptness, for their ill-preparedness. Rather, when a student was not performing, Ted and the Talking Mountain staff began asking questions to find out what was going on in the person's life, and to uncover the problems that were blocking him or her. They talked among themselves in the same way—asking questions, checking to determine how they might best help. Ted's interactions with Mark and with Larry were typical of his relationships with students. The staff, working together, created an atmosphere that valued students as their primary concern.

This is not common in secondary schools and was not typical of the larger school in which he worked. I visited several other classrooms, ate lunch with the faculty, and hung out in the faculty lounge. Students were discussed in a very different way. In one of the classrooms I visited, the following exchange occurred. The teacher told the students to sit down and get to work; another teacher was in the room, and it seemed that the two of them needed time to work on something. The students apparently knew which assignment they should be working on, as no further directions were given. One of the students kept talking to himself. The teacher asked him to be quiet. The student persisted quietly. Finally the teacher roared at him to be quiet.

Tom, the student, said, "I'm thinking."

The teacher responded with overt sarcasm, "You haven't had a thought in 3 months. Try being quiet." He then turned to the other teacher and said, loud enough for the class to hear, "These are not the cream of the crop, as you can see." The other teacher glared at the students while the students rolled their lowered eyes and became quiet.

I saw several students having confrontations with teachers in the hall. In one case, I overheard a conversation where a teacher was consciously belittling a student's ability to learn. Experiences like these are common in schools. It is uncommon to see a group of five teachers communicate such a strong, positive message to students.

Participatory Decision Making

Another theme that emerged out of the Talking Mountain data was the participatory nature of the organization. The contrast between Talking Mountain organizational style and the school's was noticeable and remarkable. The general school faculty meeting consisted of a series of announcements and edicts about things the teachers must attend to. The principal demonstrated the most common teaching techniques: he lectured; he accused the staff of poor performance without discussion; he gave a pop quiz. There was no mention of students or what the school was attempting to do for them. They were only mentioned in reference to problems, and there was no discussion of the academic agenda or of instruction or of how teachers might best meet the curriculum. It seemed almost as if the administration perceived the teachers as enemies in the educational enterprise—people who had to be prodded and scolded frequently so that they would not forget what they were really there for.

By contrast, Talking Mountain meetings were conducted democratically—through group participation—and modeled the kind of instruction I saw in their classrooms. Concern for the welfare of students was constant and central to the discussion; there were continuous references to their goals and purposes and concern about whether they were accomplishing what they hoped to. Every effort was made to involve students in the decision making about the corporation and to ensure meaningful participation for them. Every issue and decision was open to discussion for staff to influence if they chose. From the length of the debates, it seemed certain that all believed that their contribution was worthwhile and valuable.

Clearly these organizations were run very differently. What is most interesting lies in the relationship between organizational style and beliefs about learning. In the traditional high school, the teachers and the students were treated as empty vessels in need of filling. Those at the top of the hierarchy—in some cases the principal, in others the teachers—provided knowledge to those who needed it. In Talking Mountain, the teachers and the students were treated as if they had expertise and experiences that were important. They were encouraged to bring their experiences to bear on decisions affecting the organization that needed to be made. Organizational structures and decision-making processes reflect beliefs and attitudes toward learning and human potential.

Practicing the Preaching

The Talking Mountain people were learning a good deal about providing leadership for other teachers. When I asked them to describe how they'd managed to be so successful in seriously changing the practice of the teachers with whom they worked, Bill answered:

> We throw out a lot of empathy. We are people who have started stuff in right unfertile grounds ourselves. We all still teach every day. We tell folks to take change in small bits—do something that'll work, something successful. We provide a guiding philosophy that is stronger, deeper than mere strategy. We are not prescriptive—we don't tell people what to do, but we provide them with a guiding vision that is good. It is a strong ethical philosophy which is deeply resourceful. It pushes us into living with what we believe in and promotes social consciousness. We believe in working with the community. We provide two kinds of resources: (1) organizations who will help with money and resources and (2) we provide a network of teachers. We work toward collegiality. Then, I guess, we are trying to be the thing we're talking about.

Surely this strong personal involvement and the fact that they practice what they preach and the sharing of personal experience without prescription have a great effect on their credibility and on their ability to understand the complexity involved in changing instruction.

Ted himself provided enormous leadership and inspired other teachers to challenge traditional strategies, even though he did not characterize himself as a leader. Although Ted frequently found the pace of change too slow because his own methods had long ago become second nature to him and, as a result, seemed relatively uncomplicated and straightforward, his passionate concern for the general condition of the classroom experience for students gave him patience enough to listen while teachers new to the methodology asked the same questions each year. Furthermore, his own classroom experience—fraught with great victories but also many common failures and shared uncertainties—gave him the grounding, the humility to hear the struggles of others and to try to do something about them.

Teacher Leadership Focused on Teaching

Clearly, when teachers took the Talking Mountain class, the focus was not administrative but firmly fixed on the day-to-day "what do we do in the classroom" business of teaching. That emphasis on what teachers are actually primarily interested in—motivating students to better learning—provided a powerful example of teacher leadership.

In order to further develop participating teachers' and their own understanding about what they were trying to do, the Talking Mountain staff were constantly asking teachers to describe their experience with experiential education, much of which was published in *Teachers Talk*. This is a journal for teachers written by teachers and their students and published by the corporation.

In the journal a great deal of information was collected from teachers on changing their own instruction. In addition to the journal, the Talking Mountain staff frequently brought teachers together to evaluate and to discuss the difficulties and the benefits of changing their curriculum and their instruction. As a result of that ongoing evaluative dialogue, their approach to working with teachers on changing practice was constantly emerging, constantly being shaped by the teachers who were participating. Still, in all areas—teaching courses, asking teachers to write, bringing teachers together to reflect—the primary focus was on the examination of what constitutes powerful learning for students.

Winning Support

Ted won support from all of the teachers I talked with and from the community in which he lived—no small feat. In retrospect, it appears that he won that support in a step-by-step fashion. He first won the students, then the community—and a tough community at that. Wilmer is a conservative and isolated community that does not take well to outsiders, and yet he managed to come in from the outside (although he is a native of the state) by dignifying their local culture rather than trying to change it. From there, it seems that he won the respect of his colleagues—a tremendous challenge, because teachers who range out of the ordinary are often shunned by the rank and file.

With the teachers, he was perceived as a leader by everyone—even those people who he believed did not like his work. They seemed to see him as an advocate and a voice for all teachers. There was none of the professional jealousy spoken of so often by the other teachers with whom I had worked. Furthermore, none of the teachers in his school made the kinds of comments I had heard in other schools about the teachers who held leadership positions. Ted did not hold a formal role and so did not challenge the traditional egalitarian ethos of teaching—his work was not affecting the class size of his colleagues, nor did he have a title or privileges within the school system. He was treated no differently by the administration, and yet he clearly did have privileges. He team-taught two of his classes. He hired his own colleagues. He did not have to adhere to the strict time schedule that persists in schools—he could come late to his second-period class if demands of the business required more of his time. Often, he was out altogether, traveling—jet-setting, one might even call it, in a way that must have appeared very glamorous to many of the other teachers. He had been singled out for award after award. Still the teachers collectively supported him and believed that he was a singular leader.

It is remarkable that Ted was perceived by his colleagues as a leader yet managed to avoid the professional jealousy that usually accompanies such recognition. Speculating on possible explanations led me to three. One strong possibility may lie in Ted's description of himself. His first love is teaching, and he communicates that clearly to his colleagues through his actions. Regardless of all the hype and whirl, he shows up for school most days in his jeans and has done so for 22 years.

> Of all the things that I do, I enjoy teaching. I don't like meetings, I don't like fund raising, I don't like running things. I don't like run-

ning all over the county like some kind of a Johnny Appleseed. I like to teach. If they took that away from me, it would be like tak-ing oxygen away. I couldn't survive.

A second possibility stems from other teachers' perceptions of Ted as a visionary teacher. They frequently spoke of the privilege of working with him. Several treated him like a celebrity. Ted ignored any kind of adulation. He just simply never recognized it or re-sponded to it in any way. His actions, then, communicated that any teacher so compelled could teach the way he did; any teacher could help lead toward better quality instruction in the classrooms of our schools.

The third possibility might be that Ted never attacked the way teachers teach in general. He never used sweeping phrases about how lousy most classrooms are in America. When working with teachers, he shared his own personal journey with students. He described his own struggles with their inattentiveness, with their disengagement. When thinking about using new techniques, he re-flected on his own understanding of the need to change. He also talked about his personal fears and uncertainties. This approach did not affront teachers but rather pulled them into his experience.

Ted's case was at once powerful and problematic. It was prob-lematic because it was unique. His leadership role was entirely of his own making, dependent on his personal experiences with his stu-dents. It had not been planned with great care but evolved each year out of the collaboration between Ted and the participating teachers. As a result, as an example of a type of teacher leadership in current practice, it was unrelated to most of the leadership roles that are common in today's schools.

On the other hand, his role was powerful because it demon-strated what individual teachers could do to improve education if given the freedom within the existing system to build on their own successes with students and the flexibility to pursue various ways of working. It was powerful for me personally because it helped me to understand what Sizer (1984) means when he talks about schools that foster a tone of decency and unanxious expectation. Students in Ted's school were asked to choose a project that would prove mean-ingful for them. The students, year after year, met deadlines and turned out impressive projects that the community valued. They were expected to follow through and they did. It made me think about the kinds of expectations we communicate to students when we ask them to engage in learning material that is unrelated to anything else, much less their lives. In addition, the students and their work were treated with the utmost respect by the Talking Mountain teachers. Their concerns and fears were attended to by teachers who listened and responded with care—as Ted did to the student who was worried about the college entrance exams. I was struck by the connection between typical faculty room conversations where kids are not infrequently disparaged, ridiculed, or blamed for teachers' frustrations and the corresponding ways students are treated in classrooms. Ted's fellow teacher who told the student to be quiet because he hadn't had a thought in years was one of those I overheard complaining to colleagues in the faculty room about how lazy the students are. The Talking Mountain teachers didn't talk about students like that out of the classroom, and they didn't talk like that to them in the classroom. Their exchanges were decent, respectful.

Ted's case was also powerful because of its clear focus on providing more powerful learning experiences for students. It was refreshingly easy to see that students were making positive gains. I watched videotapes, listened to radio programs produced by students in his school, read articles kids had written. And the products were equally as inspiring from the students of teachers who were participating in the outreach network. I watched a videotape a kindergarten class had written, directed, starred in, and produced about the first day of school. They did it to reduce the fears future first graders were sure to feel. Their teacher absolutely beamed while the tape rolled for a group of teachers. I listened to a cassette tape produced by middle school students in the South who had recorded the work of local traditional musicians. Their teacher cornered me at one of Ted's meetings, sold me a tape, and launched into a lengthy discussion about the process the kids had gone through in order to make this recording—from getting a loan from the bank, to testing the sound equipment in the recording studio, to designing the cassette cover. These products gave me tangible evidence that Ted's work was making a powerful difference not only in the lives of teachers but in the lives of students as well.

CHAPTER 4

GWEN INGMAN
A Teacher Leader in a Principal's Model

Teacher leadership means that a teacher is able to have the power to influence policy, curriculum and procedures within the individual school and the school district. It means teachers having responsibility for instruction of children, peers, evaluation of their peers and of administrators to influence what happens in schools.
—Gwen's Colleague

THE CONTEXT

Gwen Ingman is in her 10th year of teaching in a small school district that is in the midst of transition from rural to suburban in the northwestern United States. In recent years, the surrounding cities have grown closer and closer to the quiet, green valley in which the school district rests. The urban sprawl has brought with it all the problems of a district in transition. Growth is occurring faster than the state building allocations, so while new schools are being planned, the existing buildings are full to exploding. Teachers' workrooms are shrinking to make room for specialists so that classrooms can be freed up for expanding numbers of kids. Portables dot the playground. Hiring is at an all-time high, and district personnel lament the lack of qualified teachers rather than the teacher shortage so often discussed in the news. Student populations are changing, too—blacks, Hispanics, and Asians are joining the limited number of Native American students, so that Gwen's school has its first sprinkling of color. Parent meetings reflect the blending of old locals and new suburb seeking yuppies; some work for burgeoning technological firms, whereas others are employed in the traditional, if suffering, occupations—logging, fishing, paper production.

Education, then, is important to some of the populace but not well supported by others. The superintendent plays a high-profile role in the community. He has been with the district for 6 years. He is proud of the several years he spent in the East doing doctoral work and being a principal in a large suburban system, and attributes to that experience his interest in school reform. He runs a "tight ship" in which he and his administrative council—building principals and the few central office administrators—have developed several projects and programs to promote improved instruction. In order to juggle the budget to allow for experimental programs, the superintendent negotiated with the principals to take on extra responsibility for curriculum and instruction, if he provided them with additional secretarial support. As a result, he eliminated one major salaried position, which freed a substantial sum of money for new programs. The superintendent reorganizes and experiments frequently while making the majority of the decisions.

His reform projects have varied from building-based programs to district-wide innovations, all focused on improving the quality of instruction. For instance, one elementary school is a model school for cooperative learning. Teachers in this building have worked and continue to work with university researchers who lead in this field in order to learn thoroughly how to implement cooperative learning strategies in the classroom. Another of those programs is the instructional support teacher (IST) program, which was created in response to the national call for expanded leadership roles for teachers and to the need for improved instructional techniques among teachers. Funds were committed so that each building could release one teacher half time to provide instructional support for the rest of the teachers. These support teachers were to spend their time in classrooms helping their colleagues to implement the teaching practices described in Hunter's (1976) program, Instructional Theory Into Practice (ITIP). Dr. Hunter has been a consultant in the district for a number of years, conducting in-service and working with principals and teachers. She was strongly supportive of these roles because of her experience, which has led her to believe that teachers do not change classroom behavior unless they have the opportunity to practice and to receive feedback. The leadership positions were designed to provide these opportunities—the IST could watch experimental lessons, give nonevaluative feedback, and model particular techniques when asked.

The teachers' reaction to the program was not what the superintendent expected. He believed that he had created positions that would be received enthusiastically because they responded to the need for expanded leadership opportunities for teachers and would allow teachers to collaborate on instruction. The union complained that the IST positions increased class sizes of the rank and file. Teachers were angry that they had not been consulted about the need, the design, or the implementation of these positions. Principals reported that the people selected to fill the roles were not often welcome in their colleagues' classrooms. The superintendent was disappointed and deflated by the response but believed that the positions were important to the development of instruction; so he negotiated with the local association, reaching an agreement that the positions could reflect the needs of the individual building staffs—in other words, building staffs could interpret the positions as needed in their particular context. As a result of this truce, the positions had been in place for several years with only a few complaints from the union. When I entered the district, administrators were highly supportive of the positions and believed them to be on the cutting edge of change in the teaching profession.

The context of Gwen's individual building models the larger district operations. The principal, Vivian Hebbard, has been in education for 30 years. A trim, spare woman who marches with a personal efficiency, she has been a principal in several school districts. This is her second building in this district; it houses approximately 600 children. She is a woman who is very enthusiastic about her job, very proud of her building and of her teachers. She, like the superintendent, is a great believer in educational improvement and believes that schools have come a long way in her own career. She has watched the principal's role turn from that of manager to instructional leader. As an instructional leader, she spends the majority of her time coaching teachers in clinical supervision, based on Hunter's theories of instructional improvement. Vivian is well respected by her staff for her own skill in coaching them toward better instruction.

Vivian organized the school so that it could run efficiently whether she was there or not. Several of her approaches were unconventional in elementary schools. For instance, the secretary, Frances, worked as Vivian's personal secretary and, as such, was not available to the teachers. Frances did not respond to teacher requests, seldom dealt with children, and guarded the telephone as if it were her personal property. As a result, the front office of the school had quite a different tone from that in most elementary buildings. The teachers did not congregate there to catch up; there was no children's artwork on the wall; different aides greeted the public as they came in each day. It is much more like a business office than the center of the school. Teachers were appointed to be the principal when she was away, and everyone knew exactly who it was on what days, so that business proceeded as usual. The delegation of duties went further. Teachers had assignments to arrange assemblies, to investigate particular areas of the curriculum, to arrange parent meetings, to coordinate the volunteers. Everyone agreed that Vivian was very good at delegation.

Vivian firmly believed in the IST positions and handpicked the people who served in the IST role in her building.

> I come from a strong belief that everybody can't be a coach. Takes personality plus ability. The superintendent wanted the coaches to broaden out—some have changed from coaches to gophers and administrative assistants. I've tried very hard not to do that. I've watched these people for a long time before asking them to take these positions. In both cases the staffs I have worked with have been supportive of these positions. We've worked hard to maintain a clean position.

Vivian believed that the success of these positions rested partially on the work she did to build the credibility of the person chosen to be the IST.

> I am very careful about whom I select. I have to be able to trust them. I build their credibility with the rest of the staff by having

them help me with our in-service. I have them help me with staff positions. Gwen and I planned for a team of teachers to help with in-service. We then planned the peer coaching program and aligned it with the Tactics (thinking skills) program.

When I asked Vivian if she thought the teachers should be involved in selecting the person for the IST position, she responded by saying, "No, I don't. I don't think that they've had the training nor are they selective. I've had experience since 1966 and I still don't always make good choices." Vivian notes that the application process is rigorous. "We talk about the job description. We interview for it. We post it. Applicants have to have had clinical supervision—they have to meet the criteria."

One of the reasons that Vivian believed so strongly in these positions stemmed from her assessment of how well they were working.

I assess the success of the program by staff feedback and by observing the classrooms. I listen in in the staff room. If I see these things—monitoring, individualizing, giving frequent feedback—in the classroom, then I know we're helping. We have several people who have really improved. Margie Frank had some problems, but now she doesn't.

Vivian, like the superintendent, believed in establishing a climate of improvement and was very good at delegating responsibility, but again, like the superintendent, she believed that she must take primary responsibility for the decisions made. In her own building, although teachers were very involved in a variety of projects designed to improve instruction, she made the important decisions.

THE PERSON

Gwen is a tall, neat, upbeat person in her mid-30s. She has short, brown hair and a lovely smile. She is an attractive person; she looks somewhat formal in that she is very neat—she exudes a kind of precision. At times she is a person who radiates life. She has the big, booming voice of an organizer as she sends children into their appropriate lines for the bus ride home or jokes with the students on the playground at recess—brisk, and full of energy. At other times, she is quiet, analytical, no nonsense. She has blue eyes that, in either role, are constantly moving, surveying the school to ensure orderly behavior, smooth transitions from place to place. Gwen seems to have a natural talent for ordering the movement of large groups of students, and it is a skill she enjoys exercising. She can look at a classroom and tell how the furniture disrupts the flow of business. She looked at the library and reorganized it for greater spatial utility. She moved students in and out of assemblies with a minimum of disruption. Her organizational skills and her personal efficiency are admired by the rest of the staff. Initially, Gwen appears to be like her principal—upright, organized, efficient, and neat.

An ambitious, change-oriented person, Gwen is at the same time conscientious of and proud of her own role as a teacher. At the time of this study, she was enrolled in course work to get her principal's credential and her master's degree. She was questioning whether she wanted to leave the classroom or maintain some contact with kids, as she had done in her current role as a teaching librarian. Gwen is in her 10th year of teaching. Her first 2 years were served in another state, and she often mentioned that her current district was far more enlightened and supportive of teachers than the previous district had been. Gwen's experience demonstrates that she enjoys change. She first taught special education for moderately disabled children, then went to a regular education classroom, then switched grade levels two more times. When I met her, she was a teaching librarian half time and an IST half time. As a teaching librarian, she instructed half of the students in the school in half-hour periods, once a week. She presented lessons that helped students to learn to use the library. As an IST, she had afternoons free to coach other teachers. She had been invited, at the time of the study, to consider another change to the assistant principal position, which was just being created in the school. Her wide experience at different grade levels and in both special education and regular education put her in good stead with other teachers.

As the IST for her building, Gwen had afternoons free to visit other teachers' classrooms to help strengthen their skills related to ITIP. Vivian believed that Gwen should be visiting five teachers per week, writing up the observations, and then postconferencing with the teachers. Because the observations made in this position were not connected to evaluation, feedback from the observations was strictly confidential and could be handled in any way that suited both the teacher and Gwen. The teachers agreed that Gwen could feel free to drop in at any time, so she gave them no prior notice. Gwen had had a number of courses in ITIP, both from Dr. Hunter and from other local trainers. In addition, she taught a course in beginning ITIP herself, and, as a result, felt well qualified to conduct observations. Gwen believed that ITIP techniques were appropriate to all kinds of teaching and all kinds of teacher styles. She believed that the position was designed to help all teachers to improve rather than weak ones only. Gwen spoke positively about the teachers in her school; she liked them and was proud of the things they were doing.

In addition to observing teachers, part of her IST responsibility was to help Vivian organize staff in-service during faculty meetings. This year, Gwen had organized the peer coaching project for the staff, which involved introducing the staff to the Tactics Thinking Skills program, helping Vivian assign peer coaching partners, scheduling the teachers and the substitutes during a 3-day period, and sharing the evaluation with the staff. A variety of other responsibilities came with the position, one of which was to take her turn as the designated principal in Vivian's absence. Gwen shared this responsibility with one of the male teachers.

She spent the other half of her day as a teaching librarian. After years of struggle in this district, the elementary teachers had finally won the right to a planning period several times a week. Their planning time was covered by the music specialist, the physical education specialist, and the librarians. Gwen split the responsibility for the library with Jane, a half-time kindergarten teacher. She and Jane worked together well and enjoyed the opportunity to collaborate. Together, they determined how the library should run, who would handle the media equipment and the computers, who would order the books and get them ready for shelving. In the long run, their collaboration consisted of dividing up the labor for greater efficiency. They also coordinated the parent volunteers who worked in the library. Jane and Gwen shared an office and were both free to work together on Friday afternoons. During the rest of the week, each taught half the students in the school in half-hour increments. Jane had the primary students and Gwen the intermediates. They spent a good deal of their limited time together in their office discussing problem students, the library budget, and the endless series of duties that come with running a library. Neither had had any training in library science, but both worked hard to create a working library rather than a study hall sort of place where students came to goof off.

> We wanted this to be a place where kids could feel safe. Where they could get away from the noise and confusion. We wanted a place where kids could use their research skills. Originally we wanted to have a fun place too, and so we brought costumes in for the little kids to play with under the loft. We foung that that wasn't consonant with the purpose of the library.

I seldom saw either of them sit idle; they were always laminating book covers, shelving, rearranging, replacing overhead-projector light bulbs, or cataloguing new books.

As part of her library responsibility, Gwen was specifically in charge of scheduling and working with intermediate students and teachers, managing the audiovisual equipment, checking the weekly film orders and making sure that they were all returned to the regional center on Fridays; running all school-wide assemblies and the monthly awards assemblies, organizing and presiding over bus duty, and coordinating the school-wide parent volunteer luncheon. Many of her extra assignments interfered with the time she had to function as the IST. Furthermore, "Vivian believes that the library is the hub of the school. Meetings are held here and we constantly have to work around that schedule which disrupts our working with kids." For all of her responsibilities within the school, Gwen was paid a regular teacher's salary.

Finally, Gwen held two other major leadership roles in her life outside school. She was the regional coordinator for children's programs for her very large church. In this capacity, she supervised five directors, each of whom had primary responsibility for particular kinds of programs run across the state. In addition, she was the director of children's programs for her local church. In both capacities, Gwen held a good deal of responsibility and dedicated a significant amount of time out of school to these programs.

A DAY WITH GWEN

It is April in the country. Gwen's school is surrounded by green fields, blooming trees, and a few grazing cows. On the way there, however, one can almost watch the city slowly moving in. I pass through two new shopping centers and by several new housing developments ranging from the ostentatious to the ordinary. The school itself is removed from the urban sprawl and looks to have been built in the 1950s—a rambling concrete campus with play-grounds surrounded by farms and fields.

Gwen is in the library office already, making coffee and filling the drawer with the week's supply of goodies—cookies, crackers, herbal teas—that she shares with Jane, the other half-time librarian, the parent volunteers, and the students-of-the-week who are re-warded for good behavior during recess. It is a well-lighted, very orderly space. Both Jane and Gwen have desks there and bulletin boards on which calendars, favorite sayings, and a few jokes are pinned. The weekly schedule holds a prominent place. There are several work spaces—a typewriter, a laminator, cupboards for sup-plies, and files for new book cataloguing. The school psychologist comes in to use the telephone, so Gwen goes into the library, taking her lesson plans. She grumbles, not at the school psychologist—he needs to use the telephone in privacy to make calls to parents—but at the continuous interruptions of her work by the inevitable array of people who need to telephone. Because people are constantly dis-couraged from using the telephone in the office, she has asked repeatedly to have another one put in the faculty room, but is told that the situation will be remedied when the district determines whether it is going to remodel the overcrowded school. Still, she notes that it is very difficult for the teachers to take care of any business—either personal or professional—during the working day because they have no adequate access to a telephone.

In the library, she arranges her notes for the day and checks through the overdue book file. Two girls come in, and she imme-diately stops them. "There have been some serious problems here, girls. You've given me two different stories about working on the computer." They respond in voices so low I can't hear them, to which Gwen replies, "Ms. Davis [Jane] did not say that. You can work if completely quiet." The girls look as if they'd like to argue, but Gwen has a very firm, no-nonsense demeanor. Three other girls walk in. "Come in, girls. Check out a book and read quietly. The computer's in use. Get a book and read. Wandering is not an option." Gwen goes back to the overdue book file and organizes these according to the classes she will teach during the day so she can remind the students who have forgotten their books.

The library is a large, blue space that is divided into different learning centers. Just near the door, there is a large wooden loft complete with pillows and beanbag chairs. It was originally designed as a quiet place for students to go to read and relax. Gwen notes that students use it more as a place to visit and goof off. In another part of the room, there is a carpeted, sunken, seating alcove that is used for presentations and for oral reading. Another section is arranged with round tables and chairs to accommodate a class. There is a portable blackboard on one side and freestanding bookshelves around the other sides. Along a far wall, there are three Apple II computers and a printer. The entire room is framed with bookshelves. There are several trade posters on the wall: "Reading Is Fun!" "Make a Book Your Buddy." On top of the freestanding bookshelves are student science projects: natural environments created in miniature in cardboard boxes. One wall holds examples of student work done in the library. The checkout desk is organized near the door to facilitate student traffic. Gwen completely reorganized the space to provide a better, more efficient working environment. This, like the library office, is a very neat, functional environment.

Shortly before the day formally begins, Gwen races off to the staff room for a few minutes. There is a birthday today. Each person on staff takes responsibility for celebrating one staff member's birthday, buys a present, and brings a cake or some other treat. People pass in and out, wolfing down a slice of cake while calling out aging jokes and kind insults to the birthday girl. Gwen joins a few other teachers for a minute with a cup of coffee before racing back to the library. They mention that they like working together, that they team up on projects frequently, that this is a good place to work. They visit about the present given today—a basket with perfumes, soaps, and powders in it—and compare it to what they received. As they prepare to leave they laugh about whether they should go to the bathroom or whether they should hold it. "How long can we hold it?" What kind of capacity does your bladder have?" There is only one set of staff bathrooms, a good 10-minute walk from parts of the school.

Gwen races back to the library through the children playing on the playground. Several yell to her and she waves. The school day formally begins with announcements over the intercom from Vivian. She reads a poem for the students entitled, "I Can; I Can't," which is about the importance of having a "can-do attitude." She talks to them about the importance of setting goals. "Each week you must write down your goals and put them somewhere where you can see them often. They will help you to remember what it is that you want to happen." Gwen and Kathy, the library aide, roll their eyes and note that Vivian does this only once a week. Next the music teacher and a couple of students lead the school in singing "This Is My Country." The singing is an old tradition they brought with them when several of the teachers transferred here with Vivian. The library is empty first thing Monday morning so that Gwen can get the films and audiovisual equipment out. She and Kathy talk about Kathy's daughter's wedding. Kathy is clearly suffering—does not want the wedding—and so pours out to Gwen, who listens and comments supportively, all the while checking equipment, laminating book covers, organizing files. A little girl comes in with a basket of books to return for her teacher. She stops to tell Gwen and Kathy that she was up very late last night watching TV with her mom, dad, and sister. Gwen says, "I'll bet that was fun," and the little one confirms that it was but that she's tired today. Gwen sends her back to class and confides, "Lots of kids come in to share such things, to talk. That little one wanted us to know that her dad was home—at least last night. Her parents are separated or at least have been. We listen when we can, but there isn't enough time." This is one of several comments Gwen made about the tension she feels between running the library and the rest of the school and spending time with and supporting children.

Soon, she moves out to the library teaching space to get ready for the day's schedule of classes—one kindergarten class she teaches to balance the load that Jane carries, one third grade, one sixth. She finds the sixth-grade students difficult, rambunctious.

They've been rough to keep in line. I have trouble getting their attention for longer than 10 seconds. They get mad when I'm gone, and I've been gone for three weeks in a row [she sees each class only once a week]. I'm trying to figure out how to win them over. I don't want them to leave with bad feelings about this place, but sometimes they bring it on themselves. They have so much energy that sometimes I want to kill them instead of like them. I tried to give them stuff that would help them get ready for junior high so I showed them a Newbury award winner film. They didn't like that—wanted something more meaty. So now I'm going to try to do the Tactics responsibility control lesson. I hope we can discuss but I don't know.

The little kindergarten students come in, lined up two by two. She sings a song with them about tiptoeing into the library. They sit on the carpeted stairs. Gwen reviews the day with them. First they need to go over the overdue list. Once they have done that, they need to look for new books for 10 minutes and check them out. Then they will reconvene to listen to a story. It is a story they had heard before and had illustrated. Today she will read the story again, and they can hold up their pictures at the appropriate part of the story. They all cheer; the day sounds great to them. Gwen calls off the overdue list while everyone sits quietly. Several children have forgotten to bring their books back. She reminds those who have forgotten their books that they will not be allowed to check out a book today. While the others move off to get new books, those with overdue books sit quietly at their desks. In a few minutes Gwen rings a bell and they all sit down at the desks with the pictures they drew in front of them. While she reads, they hold up their pictures of chickens, roosters, a cat, and a fox. They then move back down to the stairs to hear a new story. The atmosphere is kind and gentle. The children are well behaved, responsive, and clearly love the library. As they leave she selects the library person of the week, someone who has really worked well today. One little boy mutters disappointedly, "I never get any awards." They file out waving good-bye to Gwen.

She immediately gets ready for the next group that is at the door with the teacher before she has time to finish straightening up. She writes on the board: "What is one thing you want the students at Miller Elementary to remember about this year's sixth-grade class?"

This is the sixth-grade group. They file in noisily and sit around the round tables. Their teacher disappears in order to do his own planning. Gwen spends considerable time getting the students to attend. "Darren, is that a good place for you to sit?"

"I've been sitting here for 4 weeks."

Someone else yells, "Where's Jon been? We've been getting along real good since he's been gone." Gwen tells them that they can help Jon be a better library student.

"Ignore him when he blurts out answers. What does he want when he does that?"

"Attention!"

"Do we want him to get it that way?"

"NO!"

She proceeds through the lesson by asking them what it is that they want to be remembered for. The lesson is constantly interrupted by disruptive students. "Brian, sit down, please. This is the second time I've asked you."

"I hate sitting down. It sucks." Brian's voice is quiet, but he sits down.

As a result, the lesson moves very slowly. She goes over the responsibility frame. The kids define required words in bored voices. She explains what they will be doing, stops to regain quiet, and proceeds through to the stages of gaining responsibility. It is a tenuous, silently negotiated truce. One group of boys shoots pencils back and forth across the table.

"Gentlemen, I don't think you've had trouble using pencils in the past."

She calls for volunteers to answer questions. The time drags for both students and teacher as she calls on a student who was not listening. Four boys at one table watch me to make sure I'm watching as they mimic snorting cocaine. They roll up pieces of paper and then sniff long lines across their desk. Eventually she dismisses the lesson after stopping four more times to gain their attention or to discipline a particular student or group. She gives them time to check out books and reminds them how to do that—quietly. The group moves off toward the bookshelves. One boy goes immediately to the newspaper stand and begins waving the paper like a flag. Three other boys follow two girls up into the loft after grabbing books off the shelf. Gwen reminds them to read silently. A couple of girls ask her advice on books to read. They have a good exchange about some of her favorite books. The kids in the loft begin to punch each other and the teacher returns to take the group back to class. No library person of the week is mentioned.

Gwen breathes a sigh of frustrated relief. She bends down to pick up pencil shavings and sunflower seeds sprinkled on the floor under one of the desks. "These are Darren's. I know it for a fact. But I'm not sure it's worth a fight." I suggest that one of the students is very bright. She responds by saying, "His problem is that he's just a character—that's all. Now, I think he's intelligent enough not to get into trouble. Darren, however, is right on the brink. I think when he gets to junior high he'll be booted out—because he's just that kind of a kid. He has a really hot temper."

The school psychologist walks back in to borrow a camera and to use the telephone. They discuss who will pay for the film. Gwen does not believe the library budget should pay for his film. He decides to ask Vivian.

A third class comes in. This time they are fourth graders who are in the gifted class. The students are bright and cheerful, full of enthusiasm. She explains that over the next couple of weeks they will be making advertisements, using the library as a resource to research their projects. She shows them a few of last year's videotaped versions. On the screen, three girls advertise detergent amidst terrific giggling and faltering. Eventually they fall to the floor as a means by which to conclude the scene. The audience laughs and talks about the kids who are on the tape. When finished, they discuss other possibilities. "Jim, are you listening? Mike? Sam? I need your full attention, because the examples are so good." She tells them that they have 3 weeks to get ready for this and then dismisses them to begin working. In a few minutes, Gwen rings the bell for quiet and asks the class to lower their voices.

Ladies and gentlemen, I need your attention please. First, your voices need to get quieter. Second, who's going to be library person of the week? I appreciate that you are having fun getting your books, but the noise level is too high. There are other people working in the library, and we are trying to talk and it is difficult with the noise level. I will allow you to choose your own books if you will monitor your voice levels.

The kids scurry off to select books quietly. They primp and preen more than usual; it is school picture day for them.

It is now lunchtime. Another teacher comes in to use the phone. All the lines are busy, so she sits and waits. She and Gwen talk about the rottenness of the phones—how hard it is for them to do any planning at all without phones. This particular teacher wants to call a parent and her insurance agent. Jane races in to get ready to begin her shift of teaching in the library. They discuss the fact that they have $2,400 of Chapter II money and must determine how to spend it soon. Jane mentions a student in her class who is driving her nuts. She made him sit by the door today. "He's really smart, he makes good connections—but he's such a snot!" Gwen sympathizes and makes sure that she and Jane are scheduled to sit down together on Friday.

She races into the faculty room and joins a group of teachers. They discuss problem students and note that it has become much more difficult to teach these days because the home life of their students is so unstable. Too many pressures, too much curriculum, not enough time. Gwen is interrupted by the secretary who informs her that Child Protective Services (CPS) is coming concerning a suspected child-abuse case. According to the guidelines she is reading, Gwen will need to be present in Vivian's absence. The topic at the lunch table moves on to gardening and how difficult it is to keep up with lawns at this time of the year. Everyone reveals a solution for dealing with the problem. Several people discuss a district scandal no one is supposed to know about (clearly, everyone does!) prior to moving back to their classrooms. The sixth-grade teacher walks through and several teachers tell him how good his class was today. He grins and says, "Jon is gone." Jon is one of the more difficult students mentioned earlier by his students during their time with Gwen in the library. Gwen pours another cup of coffee and explains that she takes an additional 10 minutes because she does not get morning recess. She and I talk about how she was selected for the IST position, what it had been like for her, and how she and the staff had negotiated her work with them.

They said I was the most qualified. I had had clinical supervision. However, some people have not had it who have been given the position. I have been loyal—loyal to the principal, the building, the stability. I think you had to have taken some extra steps towards personal growth—classes, working on another degree. Most everyone I've known has had successful teaching experience. My first year was spent proving myself to the other teachers. I really worked hard in their classrooms to make sure that they made growth towards success. When I first introduced myself, I felt the negativism. The teachers thought maybe the position was for spying. Vivian was new here then too and the staff didn't know how to approach her. I spent a lot of my time as a liaison between the staff and the principal. I bought a lot of doughnuts that year . . . just to build that trust. There has never been any formal discussion with the staff that I know of about the role of the IST. This year the association has picked it up. They sent out a questionnaire asking something like, "Would you rather have another prep period per week in lieu of the IST position?" What are people going to say to a question like that? Vivian says that the administrators are really standing firm behind the positions though.

A sub comes in to announce that she really had to deal with a rotten kid. Gwen explains the procedures for dealing with discipline problems, and then notes under her breath how difficult it is to deal with all the subs. Because they often bring their classes into the library, Gwen ends up dealing with their problems—another thing that prevents her from attending to all of her other responsibilities. I ask her how her position is evaluated. Gwen notes that there is no formal evaluation system that she knows of. She evaluates her own success on a daily basis.

There are days when I can say that I've helped several people. Sometimes I help three or four kids. Those kinds of days make me feel that the position is viable. But then there are those days when I have to get ready for assemblies or fill out forms all day; then I think those days that it's not worth it. I feel like I've gotten nothing done.

We walk along the corridors to do an observation. Gwen does not schedule her visits, she drops in. The staff has agreed that this is okay. Gwen bases her observations on Dr. Hunter's philosophy that 2- to 3-minute walk-throughs are adequate to get a feeling for the instruction. Gwen finds that she needs between 10 and 15 minutes and tries hard to be unobtrusive in her entrances and exits from classrooms. Although she has noted that there has been no open discussion among staff members about the focus of the observations or the ways in which feedback should be given, she generally looks for the objective of the lesson, the level of difficulty for the students, the teacher's ability to monitor and adjust the lesson, and active participation on the part of the students. (In my conversations with her, she did not appear concerned that the faculty had not been involved in any kind of discussion about how the IST role worked; rather, she indicated that it was the normal procedure in the district.) She has made recommendations to teachers on how to use ITIP more effectively, although not as frequently as she would like because she feels that it is important in her nonevaluative role to wait for people to ask for feedback.

As we approach one classroom doorway, I can see that all of the children are on the floor, on all fours in a circle. Heads are down and rear ends are up. It is difficult to locate the teacher, and everyone seems intent on something that must be in the center of the circle but out of our range of vision. Gwen veers away from the doorway before entering, explaining that ITIP coaching works best with direct instruction, teacher-centered instruction, so that she would rather come back on a day when the teacher is conducting the lesson. She explains that they are investigating a turtle, and that things can get a little wild while they are doing those kinds of unstructured activities. Because she takes verbatim data on what teachers say and do, this kind of lesson is not so appropriate for her observations.

We go into Mr. Sawyer's room. He is teaching third graders a math activity. To begin, they are playing a game where students race up to his desk when they get the right answer. The racing seems to take the place of the buzzer in a college bowl kind of game. He then moves to a timed math quiz after calling for quiet. Gwen sits in the back of the room and takes notes on a yellow pad. The timing begins. After a few minutes, he yells, "Stop!" There is much cheering and groaning. He says, "You'll make it. You're doing well. I have confidence. All you have to do is get there and there'll be a treat." He then has the students take out their math books. "If you want to do this together, we can. If you choose to visit, then you'll have to do the problems in the book by yourselves." Gwen puts a note on his desk and we leave. The observation lasted for approximately 8 minutes.

From his room, we move to the art specialist's room. Linda teaches all the children in the school from a portable that is too hot in the summer and too cold in the winter and has no storage space for materials and the inadequate supplies. She struggles cheerfully against the odds, having chosen to move from teaching at the community college level to elementary. Gwen observed one of her classes earlier in the preceding week, and so their objective today is to debrief. The lesson involved having children hold up instruments during a song. The music teacher was attempting to teach two things—the identification of specific instruments and familiarity with a particular musical form. They settle in with a little chitchat first.

GWEN: How did you feel about that lesson?

LINDA: They were most inattentive. It was fun, but I wish they'd picked it up sooner. They had to identify two things and, eventually, they got them.

GWEN: You use your time so efficiently in 30 minutes. One thing I noticed yesterday. You used that song in about five different ways. You showed the kids what a ballad is. You identified particular instrument sounds within the ballad. You showed them the rhythm and the beat of the ballad . . . and you did all of that in such a short period of time!

LINDA (pleased): Now I'm faster. And I understand the kids better. They sit across from each other. I have them raise their hands when I call out a particular instrument.

GWEN: You focus them well. You changed one part which enabled you to do more. You had all the kids involved.

LINDA: I have them do that so I can understand where they are, and so I can watch those two kids. I promised them that if they give me a signal, I won't call them on it if it's wrong. I just want them to participate.

GWEN: Some kids had wrong answers but they were answering. Only thing is—might be your time constraint—you obviously wanted them to understand shapes. You could have extended that discussion.

LINDA: Yes, I could have tied it to Africa, too.

GWEN: That in itself is a good extension.

LINDA: It is a time constraint—I can't do as much with each group or lesson as I'd like. We have so much to cover.

GWEN: Are you closer this year [to covering the curriculum]?

LINDA: Yes. And I'm sure I'll get better.

GWEN: Can you see pieces [of the curriculum] to eliminate?

LINDA: No, but I get better at compressing.

GWEN: You did such a nice job. Those kids walked away with a lot.

The conversation switched at this point to Linda's new house, her own children, and a son who was away at college. The conversation finished on a very positive note. They both seemed pleased and Linda was grateful for the feedback.

Gwen goes next to the library office. Jane is there and talks about a little boy who is "a pain in the ass." They tell me several stories about his poor behavior and his lack of judgment. Gwen moves to the typewriter to send off a letter to confirm the fall faculty retreat, another of her responsibilities as the IST. A student, 10-year-old Molly, comes in and pleads to help. Gwen hands her a rag and says she can dust off the shelves. Gwen has several library aides who come in to help. As Jane goes out to teach a class, Gwen turns back to the retreat planning. Toward the end of the period, she grabs her coat and a series of signs and heads out to marshal the buses.

Previously she noted that kids were racing to the buses from every which direction and that it was very confusing for some children, so she devised a system where all the teachers participate in helping the kids to line up according to their bus numbers. Each teacher represents a particular bus number, and the children line up behind the corresponding teacher. We wait while the kids line up. A little girl twists and turns and says to me in a voice loaded with sarcasm beyond her size, "Do you like the way we acted?" When the line seems complete and orderly, Gwen holds up a sign with a particular bus number on it and dismisses the children to board their bus. The system seems to work well and allows the teachers to check to make sure that their students are where they are supposed to be. Several times I see the teachers notice that someone is missing or direct a child to the right place.

As the buses leave the grounds, teachers begin filing into the library for a faculty meeting. Friends cluster around tables, and everyone chats quietly. Vivian chairs the meeting, convened to discuss student awards. (Awards assemblies are held once a month. Gwen organizes them and parents are invited.) Gwen has commented to me on the way to the meeting that the assemblies have really gotten out of hand; parents send flowers to their children at school and make a really big deal about it, and the awards assemblies eat up a lot of instructional time.

Vivian tells the staff that she would like to reach consensus about awards for students and then proceeds to ask everyone on the faculty for an opinion. The opinions range. Some teachers believe that it is important for kids to receive an award at an assembly; others do not. Some believe that it does more harm than good because it creates an elite group. Gwen says, "I don't give awards in the library and so I don't have an opinion here." Vivian says that they have established a policy that every student will receive an award for something well done, for some success. She goes on to say that there is a ton of research indicating that awards do make a difference in student motivation. "I would like you all to check to make sure that there are enough awards available in the staff workroom. I want you to take this seriously." Vivian asks everyone to vote for or against awards, collects the voting papers, and moves on to the next topic; apparently Vivian feels a consensus on rewards has been achieved.

The staff meeting turns to announcements: the next staff meeting and guarding keys. Gwen then reports on the peer coaching evaluations gained from staff. She organized the peer coaching program, as mentioned previously, around the Tactics Thinking Skills curriculum so that each teacher was observed and had the opportunity to observe another teacher teaching. The teams were selected by Vivian and Gwen and crossed grade levels. No formal evaluations were done, but comments were collected from staff. Gwen notes that people seemed to enjoy the coaching opportunity, but that she could not tell whether they preferred the cross-grade-level teams. She reports that several people commented that they could see real similarities between grade levels. She offers the faculty another sign-up sheet if they want to be involved again on a voluntary basis without the benefit of substitute-covered release time, and she hands out an article on peer coaching.

Vivian then turns the meeting's focus to the earthquake drill. They discuss the drill at length. A parent presents information on the annual fun run. Vivian announces the date of the staff barbecue, and the meeting is concluded. It is late in the afternoon. Gwen returns to her office to straighten up and to get organized for the next day. She anticipates a busy afternoon because a neighboring junior high school band is coming to perform for two assemblies. Gwen is in charge of organizing all of the electrical equipment, the schedule, the seating, and so forth. Behind her the pile of books to be prepared for shelving reminds her that there is other work to do. She leaves around 5 p.m., in time to eat dinner before another evening meeting at the church.

OTHER RESPONSIBILITIES

On other days, Gwen's schedule varied. Her first priority was to be prepared for her classes and to make sure that students and teachers used the library well and appropriately. The rest of her time was prioritized according to the events of the day and the principal's schedule. She spent one day dealing with discipline problems when the principal was out, part of another in a meeting with a parent concerning his child who had been assigned to special education classes. For the better part of another day she untangled a district edict to have the children experiment with voting machines. (The superintendent announced at the principals' meeting that each of the schools would participate in National Voter's Week. This was in April, toward the end of the school year when most of the teachers felt pressure to rush through the already overcrowded curriculum. Students were to practice using historical characters in real voting machines. The staff was covertly furious.) She coordinated assemblies, covered classes for teachers who had doctors' appointments, organized in-service, helped other ISTs with special projects, attended district-wide meetings, replaced light bulbs, covered books, arranged schedules for the library volunteers, conferenced with the principal, and planned end-of-the-year luncheons. In addition, she was the school test coordinator and so organized the standardized testing at several grade levels and ordered all other tests needed. In the 2½ weeks that I was in the school, Gwen conducted eight observations of teachers in her building. Of those, she had feedback sessions with two. One took place several days after the observation. The other took place seven working days later and had to be rescheduled three times because both she and the teacher were very busy. In the case of the other six teachers, Gwen left notes on their desks that she felt sufficed as feedback.

HER COLLEAGUES

"All positions which exist are advisory to the administration and powerless."

"All positions/opportunities are advisory to the administrators. They are very superficial and unempowered. They are not truly leadership roles."

—*Two of Gwen's Colleagues*

While in Gwen's school, I interviewed another four people—a strong supporter, someone who Gwen believed did not either wildly support or reject her role, the Association representative, and someone who did not find the position useful. Her predictions were not totally accurate in that the four divided into two nonsupporters, one who was supportive because she believed that the role might enable her, the teacher, to share her techniques with others and another who felt that Gwen had really helped her. In all four cases, the people were reluctant to give up the time to be interviewed. In the end, Gwen volunteered to cover their classes for the time needed for the interview.

This group of interviewees was significant for a couple of reasons. Three of those I interviewed had come to education as a second career; thus, they were more knowledgeable about other occupations and more articulate than the other teachers I interviewed about the variety of ways public schools might be better organized on behalf of students. Although two of those interviewed believed that Gwen was providing meaningful support for other teachers, all four indicated that she was in an awkward position, in that she functioned as an arm of the principal. "When this position was first created, it was voluntary and part of Curriculum and Instruction. No one used the ISTs then. Then, the dictum came down that we would have the IST in." Several noted that the teachers in general resented the fact that Gwen had the authority to come into their classrooms, but that she handled it very well by being positive and supportive. They also noted that her experience with a variety of grade levels and with special education students worked to her advantage.

When asked what Gwen did in her leadership position, two teachers indicated that she gave them good feedback on the lessons they were conducting. One teacher went on to give examples of their interactions:

> One time I was having trouble with RAP Math—the room arrangement. She saw right away and changed the arrangement. It was as if I were a blind person. I think she is well placed in her role. She is a natural at being the boss of other people's kids. . . . Our discussions are never based on ITIP—they're more focused on teaching. I like to share my ideas with her because she may be able to share them with other teachers.

Another teacher described her responsibilities in this way:

> She visits classrooms and gives feedback. I don't know what she's supposed to look at—but to give us a pat on the back. She also helps with problems. She has a great deal of confidence and offers suggestions in a confident way. She has research to back her suggestions up. She conducts observations in a sensitive way. I never have felt like I was being spied on. I don't know if what she does enters evaluation, but I feel she'd be fair. She does in-service things at our staff meetings and teaches the ITIP classes. I liked the class (which is a requirement for all staff). They presented it in a nice way—that it is a tool. She really dealt with a less than cooperative group in an excellent way. They were a lot worse than third graders. She has a positive attitude towards her job and doesn't take the negative feedback personally.

The two other teachers interviewed did not feel positively about the position and its effectiveness.

> She visits classrooms. I don't see the design of what she does. I see it as random and arbitrary. If there's a structure, it's a mystery to me. I don't know what her purpose is and how she means to accomplish it. I don't know what her philosophy is or the district's.

This understanding is essential. I had no input on her role. I don't know the process of selection and so, it does not have my support. In my room she comes in for a very brief time and then, I get brief, informal, superficial feedback on what she saw. The overriding feeling of that feedback session is social. There's little criticism of the teaching—very artificial. That is not the way to get to better education. If peers are willing to accept responsibility for evaluating each other, we must roll up our sleeves and get down and dirty.

The other interviewee described the position in this way:

It is [a role as] Vivian's gopher. She picks up on administrative things Vivian can't get to. I think she could do more with curriculum, if she wanted to. Oftentimes, administrators look for the ITIP process rather than at good teaching. And I think that they often choose teachers who have trouble with kids and put them in leadership positions to relieve them of their responsibilities. I wish I could have seen her work with problem teachers. I haven't seen much improvement in one I work with. She doesn't have the power to change poor teaching. I do think that the quality of what she has to say is good. All the positions here are powerless. The administration puts teachers on committees, asks them to work on curriculum, but gives them no power to make decisions—it is a tremendous frustration.

Whereas one of her colleagues had no idea how Gwen had been selected for the position, another believed that it was done by the administrator and that that was as it should be. "Mary did it. She decided to get an all-around good teacher. I think it has to be the administrator. They are the only ones who get into all the rooms to see who's the most well rounded."

The other two had strong feelings that the process was problematic. "She applied, but only a few people did. It was hard to find people to fill the IST positions because of the class-size issue. Vivian has asked me to pursue it, but I feel that I would be betraying the rest of the teachers."

I have no idea how she was selected. I do not agree with the procedures because they were secretive, undemocratic, and totally out of my control. And yet, I get some notion that she has some influence on the way I do things.

When asked whether they believed that there should be more leadership positions in the school, all interviewed said that more IST positions would not be helpful. Three stressed that teachers needed more time to work together. Two mentioned that it would be helpful to have a resource—someone "who could help develop more effective lessons. It is hard to stay current in all of the disciplines elementary teachers have to deal with."

I would like to see someone who could do creative stuff—who could build units, who could help me do what I want and believe is best for my students. I don't have enough time to be as creative as possible for the kids.

A third teacher described several different roles:

I would start with curriculum. There should be a way that the building could focus on its own curricular goals and should have the ability to influence the district. Should be able to follow state minimums, and yet under our own steam. We should be able to meet the state Student Learning Objectives [SLOs], to revise them so that we can have a quality educational program. A group could set curriculum policy for the building in such a way that the building is more accountable. We know best what we need to teach and how. We need to determine the curriculum. Kids end up weaker for it when administrators build the curriculum. They've lost touch with kids. We'd be able to see the redundancies, find the weaknesses, etc. A second responsibility would be to allow teachers to do the school scheduling. We should sit down with the administrator and do it together. If teachers made these decisions, things might run a little bit better and more effectively for kids. And we need more time to work together. Less than 1% of our time is designed for professional exchange.

Three out of four interviewed believed that new positions should be selected by peers and that somehow or other, the role should rotate so that more people had the opportunity to work with others.

While I was in the school, several other teachers approached me to have their say about the IST position. I gathered a good deal of information on the history of the role. Everyone mentioned that the positions had been instituted as an edict and that they left whoever held them in a difficult position. All of these conversations were held out of Vivian's or Gwen's range of hearing.

CHARACTERISTICS OF PRESCRIPTIVE TEACHER LEADERSHIP

I thought about Gwen's role, like Ted's, so that I could describe it according to a set of general characteristics including its purpose, the incentives, the assumptions, the effects on students, the challenges it posed to the existing system, and the kinds of collegiality it required. Gwen's role might be called "prescriptive instructional improvement" in that it centered around a particular model of instructional improvement that included a set of identifiable behaviors—monitoring and adjusting, anticipatory set, closure, and so forth. It was also prescriptive in that the administrators in the district had identified it for the teachers. The purpose of the role was to improve instruction by educating teachers about the teaching behaviors described by Instructional Theory Into Practice. Gwen's job was to watch other teachers teach and to suggest to them how they were using the prescribed techniques, or how they might better use them to improve their teaching.

The incentives for participation in the program were negative for the larger teaching force in Gwen's building. Teachers did not have the option to participate in the program; they had been told that they would participate. The incentive for Gwen was strong in that it gave her the opportunity to tackle a new challenge, to watch a variety of teachers teach, and to have a more flexible schedule. As she was interested in administration, it also gave her a closer idea of what administrative work was like.

There were no positive effects on students that were obvious to me. Both Gwen and Vivian believed they could see improvements in teacher behaviors—teachers becoming more organized, teachers making better use of the techniques. As far as I could tell, there had been no explicit attempt to determine what effect Gwen's role might have on students. Implicitly they believed that if teachers were better organized, or using these techniques in improved ways, then students were having better experiences in the classroom.

Gwen's role required that one teacher be placed on half-time release. The only challenge this proposed to the existing system was to ensure that teachers would accept the higher teaching load. This was done at the bargaining table. The increase was so small—each teacher hypothetically took an additional one-third of a student—that it was accepted yearly by the bargaining team. In addition, Gwen's role seemed to support the existing system in that teachers were encouraged to hone traditional teaching techniques.

Mentoring was the major form of collaboration that Gwen's role fostered. Gwen, knowledgeable in the techniques made explicit by Dr. Hunter, helped other teachers to develop their skills. Because of the administrative mandate that all teachers would participate, she found herself in a forced mentoring role. While "mandated mentoring" suggests a good oxymoron, it somehow misses the intention of collaboration.

The implicit assumptions that undergird the role communicate a very different message to teachers about teaching:

1. Those higher up in the hierarchy are best suited to determine instructional methods and means for improvement. Thus, administrators select for teachers and teachers select for students.
2. All teachers can improve their instruction by focusing on a set of generic teacher behaviors.
3. Administrators are most able to identify teacher leaders and to evaluate their efficacy.
4. Teachers benefit from the teacher leader's work, which justifies increasing the pupil load of some teachers.
5. Instructional improvement occurs when a teacher leader makes brief, unannounced visits and conducts brief feedback sessions or leaves notes.
6. Teacher leaders are available for administrative support as well as for instructional improvement.
7. Students have more powerful learning experiences when teachers use a set of generic teaching behaviors.

Although these assumptions certainly were not explicit, they were understood implicitly by everyone involved. And, there was substantial disagreement with them. Although the original purpose of this role is in sync with the national call for teacher leader positions, closer examination of the general characteristics of this particular role leaves an unpleasant aftertaste.

DOMINANT THEMES

As I pondered Gwen, her role, and the context of her school and district, several dominant themes emerged. The most important theme dealt with the bureaucratic organization and the hierarchical structure of decision making in this particular school. Gwen's position illuminated the contradictions that exist between bureaucratic organizations and notions of professional responsibility with a clarity I had not previously seen.

The Effects of Bureaucratic Structures and Hierarchical Decision Making

Gwen works in a school district that is organized as a bureaucracy. Traditionally, decisions in bureaucracies are made by those who are at the top of the system. Top position holders are granted the authority to make decisions because they are often believed to have superior information and more experience within the system. In such circumstances, the decision makers seldom look for support for their decisions from those below them but rather seek the approval of the next person up the decision-making ladder. Such decision making is designed to increase the efficiency and the effectiveness of the organization. On the other hand, again by definition, professionals make decisions on behalf of their clients based on the specialized knowledge they have. Teachers consider themselves professionals and believe that they are best able to make decisions that would improve their classroom instruction because of their firsthand knowledge of their students and the curriculum. Gwen's position has its own place in the hierarchy. She decides whose classroom to visit, and how they should discuss the instruction demonstrated.

Gwen's position exemplifies the first and most problematic effect of hierarchical decision making. At least some of the teachers, claiming professional responsibility for their students, resented the imposition of a helping role about which they were not consulted. Although they liked and supported Gwen as a person, they clearly did not choose or approve of instructional assistance in ITIP as the way to improve their teaching. None of them, including Gwen, recommended that more of these positions be instituted. In addition, they all described very different kinds of positions when asked what would improve instruction while improving the nature of the teaching career.

Particularly interesting was Gwen's suggestion for additional roles. She believed that instruction could be improved by providing a wider variety of leadership positions. Her description was close to Meyer's (1971) concept of leadership density in that she described roles that would enable a large number of teachers to play to their strengths. For instance, one group of teachers was currently engaged in a search for better language arts instruction. Another teacher was really interested in understanding how computers could suport better instruction. Another was interested in social studies. Gwen believed that given some time and funding, these people could provide better support to the rest of the staff if they were given more time to work in their interest areas.

The superintendent and the principal, on the other hand, created the position and shaped it according to their own beliefs about their decision-making responsibility. They did not seek input from those who would perform the roles or from those who would be served by the roles, because it did not occur to them. As a result, in this particular circumstance, the role was strongly defended by the administrators rather than by the teachers for whom it was designed. The role itself was rendered much less effective than it might have been had the decision-making processes been different.

A second and related effect of bureaucratic decision making was that the teachers engaged in overt compliance with the teacher leadership role and then engaged in covert resistance. Although many of the teachers with whom I visited did not believe that this role supported better teaching, they were unwilling to challenge the administrative hierarchy and therefore appeared to condone the practice. As a result, the teachers assisted the principal to honestly believe that the role was working very well and that it was well supported by all. Such overt support of their decisions led these administrators to continue to operate in less than meaningful ways.

At the same time, the teachers reached some measure of negative satisfaction in that they poured the metaphorical castor oil down the sink rather than taking it or suffering the consequences of arguing about it with the resident doctor. Precisely this kind of overt support of the authoritarian structure of hierarchies has proved to be so problematic in previous attempts at reform (see, e.g., Sarason, 1971; Popkewitz et al., 1982; McNeil, 1986). From this vantage point, hierarchical decision making subverts the potential for better schools by seducing the administrators into believing in the wisdom of their own authority and by forcing teachers to behave covertly instead of overtly. Thus, both teachers and principals are in collusion as they work at cross purposes, canceling the potential to collaborate in the building of better schools.

Gwen, too, felt herself to be in—and at the same time to be a contributor to—the conundrum. As a teacher herself, she expressed resentment of the principal's wholesale authority over the role, and noted that there were a number of discrepancies between Vivian's descriptions of it and the reality of the position, but because of the hierarchical nature of decision making in the district, she felt unable to discuss her concerns with Vivian.

As a result of the practice of "top down," or hierarchical, decision making, a sort of strangling chain of fine, descriptive rhetoric and contradictory practice repeated itself through the layers of the district. The superintendent communicated building-level goals to the principals. He insisted that each school have a closely supervised IST position that would improve the quality of instruction district-wide. He then required an enormous amount of the principals' time in meetings at the central office, so that Vivian, at least, did not appear able to monitor the role in the way she had hoped. He never checked to see how his own actions confounded his own rhetoric. Vivian communicated her expectations for the role to Gwen in the same way—multiple observations and feedback sessions per week and close supervision of the IST position. Vivian told me that Gwen conducted five observations and postconferences per week; Gwen managed eight observations in 2½ weeks and only two feedback sessions. Vivian never asked for a close accounting of the observations or how the feedback sessions were going. Gwen also noted that Vivian asked Gwen to do two observations a day while I was in the building. Gwen felt that this was not only unrealistic in light of her other responsibilities, but that it would not portray the position as it really existed. Vivian never asked whether Gwen actually accomplished this. Furthermore, Vivian told me that she and Gwen met once a week to review Gwen's schedule and her work and that she observed Gwen in the act of working with other teachers. Gwen clarified that at best, she and Vivian met once a month and that Vivian had never observed her in action with the other teachers. Because of her frequent absences, Vivian seemed unable to follow through on her plans but did not gather any information that would enable her to recognize how her own actions confounded her good intentions.

Just as the superintendent thwarted her efforts, she thwarted Gwen's. Vivian outlined the number of observations and feedback sessions that should take place per week, and then required that Gwen take on a host of other administrative duties that prevented Gwen from being able to accomplish her primary tasks. Despite the fact that such delegation contradicted Vivian's very description of the role, she requested that Gwen coordinate the volunteers' tea, the regularly scheduled awards assemblies, the daily loading of the buses, the organization of the peer coaching schedule, and even more. Each of these duties was to be accomplished during the time when Gwen was observing other teachers. Not only did the delegation of additional duties confound Gwen's hope to work with other teachers, it obscured her responsibilities from the other faculty members so that they had almost no idea what she did with the bulk of her time. Vivian never requested information about how each of these responsibilities impinged on Gwen's ability to work with teachers.

In some despair, Gwen confided that Vivian did not accept criticism well, that they did not really exchange information on how this position should work. Gwen felt that she had been punished for disagreeing with Vivian before and, as a result, refrained from giving Vivian the kind of honest feedback she believed would have strengthened the viability of the position. The fact that communication moved in only one direction—from the top down—canceled the potential for the role to work. Gwen was not free to discuss how the extra responsibilities thwarted her ability to work with teachers, nor could she share with Vivian her misgivings about the utility of the observations and the feedback sessions.

Stuck right in the middle of this dysfunctional hierarchical chain of decisions, Gwen attempted to support teachers to the best of her ability by offering encouragement and suggestions when asked for them. Recognizing her lack of authority, and not wanting to incur the wrath of her supervisor, she determined to make the best of it by supporting both the teachers and the principal as best she could. Under these circumstances, she served neither the teachers nor the principal as well as she might have. She was constrained by a compromise from which neither the teachers nor the administrator nor Gwen profited.

The school's hierarchical nature had another effect on the relationships in the school. These relationships surfaced at Talking Mountain and are described in McNeil's (1986) book, *The Contradictions of Control*. McNeil suggests that the administration's values are communicated from the administrators to the teachers. In many cases, the teachers translate the same values to the students in their classrooms. As we saw in Ted Newton's school, many of the teachers treated the students similarly to the way the principal treated them. That same transference seemed to take place in this school.

The authority vested in the various place holders within the system created a kind of climate that devalued people who held lesser positions. This seemed to be pervasive throughout the school. The superintendent made the bulk of the important decisions. In our private conversations, the principal indicated that she disagreed with a number of his decisions. At the same time, the principal believed that she knew more than the teachers, and that it was her responsibility to make certain decisions for them in their best interests. She was very explicit in her beliefs in this regard when she indicated who should select teachers for positions of extra responsibility and when she determined that cross-grade-level peer coaching should take place, despite the fact that the teachers wished to coach with their grade-alike peers. The teachers both respected her and balked at the notion that she knew more about their business than they did. They did not overlook for a second the condescending nature of her beliefs. As a result, they frequently talked about her and resisted her authority among themselves.

My observations led me to believe that teachers unconsciously treated students in much the same way the principal treated the teachers. The little girl who was clearly misbehaving (according to the rules of the school) in the bus line provided a haunting example.

Her words were, "Did you like the way we acted?" but the message was quite different, "You might be able to tell us how to act, but you can't control us!" The teachers conveyed the same message to the students that the principal communicated to them: "We make the decisions here because we know best." They made the rules and to a large extent treated the students as lesser place holders. The students in return demonstrated a minimum of overt compliance with the rules and a great deal of covert disregard for the perceived authority. This was more obvious with the older students than it was with those who were younger.

There were other manifestations of how this superior/subordinate relationship played out with kids. Every day that I was in the school, I overheard the teachers engage in negative talk about students.

"That kid is a real pain in the ass!"

"There are days when I'd like to drop kick him . . ."

"Things are running smoothly because little John is absent!"

Although these kinds of comments are common in many schools, they were particularly noticeable in this one, given that it was an elementary school. Teachers did not talk about students they were proud of or students who were really making progress. The predominance of negative comments created a tone in the school that implied that children were the least valued members of the community.

The outcome of this atmosphere was clear in several of the classrooms in which I observed. Many of the teachers believed it was their responsibility to control the students and to find meaningful activities for them in order to promote learning. Because the students found themselves in a controlling environment rather than one focused on meaningful engagement, they protested by misbehaving—just at the threshold of acceptable behavior. Thus, both the teachers and the students were frustrated and disengaged from the learning process. This kind of control tension existed in a number of the classrooms—in the arts room, in the math class, in the class that was examining the turtle—and was replicated in the faculty meeting on consensus.

It is important for me to note the exceptions; not all of the classrooms I observed followed the above pattern. In a couple of cases I did observe in classrooms where children participated in decision making appropriate to their age and expertise, where the atmosphere reflected a deep respect for their knowing. Out of the 10 classrooms I visited, these were the exception rather than the rule. In a fifth-grade room, the teacher had established a student-run court system to teach them about the American judicial system. There students had a means by which to appeal homework assignments, classroom foci, and student infractions. The atmosphere in this classroom was one of partnership, and the students were taking their roles very seriously. In another instance, a teacher challenged her students in creative ways to make choices so that all students would have equal opportunity to be heard. In this room, students were working in cooperative groups that were researching global issues. Although the control tension did not exist in these classrooms, the instruction demonstrated in these rooms was not celebrated in the school at large.

Another effect surfaced again and again. The hierarchical structure of the school seemed to create a compartmentalized and competitive atmosphere in the school. The secretary competed for her turf, did not deal with students, and treated the teachers with a kind of rude disdain. The principal delegated authority to particular individuals and held the major decisions close. Many of the teachers reflected this condition by being very conscious of who had responsibility for what and by being unwilling to do something that fell into someone else's realm of responsibility. I observed numerous examples of this kind of interaction. One teacher was asked to go to a meeting of the language arts committee, but because that was out of her realm of responsibility, she chose not to go. Gwen was constantly battling with teachers over whose budget something should be taken out of, or whether she should cover a doctor's appointment or not—whether that was a legitimate part of her job description. Gwen told me about a little boy, a first grader who came to school without the proper documentation. His family had not come in to get him enrolled. Because no one was prepared to enroll him without the proper paperwork, he was left to follow her around for the entire day. The school seemed more businesslike, compartmentalized, and streamlined for greater efficiency than it did a place to nurture kids—in keeping with the image created by the superintendent and the principal. The school suffered a kind of fragmentation as a result. It was not a warm place, and there was no sense of family. Furthermore, the teachers and the staff competed for the principal's time and resources, whereas the students competed for the teachers' attention. Although individual teachers created warm settings, this was not the pervasive tone established throughout the school. Because children came to school with all kinds of personal irregularities and because they had to compete for teachers' attention, it seemed that the students frequently acted out in inappropriate ways—in order to get the attention. By behaving in this way, the kids confirmed the teachers' worst superior/subordinate suspicions.

Obviously, this particular theme illustrates a troubling paradox. In a hierarchical system, where decision making is vested in those at the top, it becomes very difficult for those at the bottom—the teachers—to make decisions on behalf of their clients. Certainly, in this case the teachers were not participants in the design or the implementation of a teacher leadership position that would improve their instruction, and were never offered the opportunity to critique or to discuss any aspect of the role. The fact that decision making moved from the top down with no attempt to involve those at lower levels of the system damned any top-down attempt at reform and provided no vehicle for any bottom-up attempt to take place.

Supporting Teacher-Centered Instruction

A second theme emerged that was perhaps the most depressing. It, too, was related to the hierarchical nature of the district. The hierarchical nature of this particular system appeared to support a predisposition toward teacher-centered instruction. Some common methods in teacher-centered instruction are lecture, teacher-directed discussion, and independent seat work monitored by teachers. Information moved from the top down in this system, as it is supposed to do in hierarchical systems. Those holding responsibility believed that they had to convey the appropriate knowledge and information to their subordinates. The most efficient method of conveying information is to lecture to the whole group, which was the predominant instructional method I observed. The principal lectured to the teachers during the faculty meeting. Only once were they asked to express their opinions, which was in regard to student awards, a situation mentioned earlier. After the opinions—both positive and negative—had been aired, Vivian concluded by saying that they had established a policy that would ensure that every student in the school would receive some award during the year. "I want you to take this seriously." One of the teachers interviewed indicated that he was well aware that they were not building consensus but being told what to do.

The principal also imparted information to the students in her morning announcements. She gave minilectures about goals and about believing in one's self. Similarly, in a majority of the classrooms I visited, the teachers provided the important information to the children. Students appeared to have few opportunities during my observations to affect the method or the substance of what they were to learn.

As an undeniable manifestation of its support of teacher-centered instruction, the district selected a teacher leadership model to bring about teachers' professional development that focused on teacher behaviors in whole-group instruction. All teachers in the district were required to take a district-sponsored course that taught teachers to create a "set," to monitor and adjust, to establish closure. Although it is true that the district supported other instructional models, as indicated by the school that was involved in cooperative learning, the fact that they required a class in these techniques for all district personnel communicated pretty clearly which behavior was more valued.

Gwen, who had had a substantial amount of training, described her position as designed so that she focused her attention on teacher behaviors. She admitted that she did not generally observe experiential activities nor did she do her observations on days when the teacher was not central to the learning taking place, because the techniques she was helping people to acquire required more teacher-centered activities.

Teacher-centered methods are, in fact, the most commonly used in schools across the country at all levels of the educational system (see Goodlad, 1984; Sizer, 1984; Boyer, 1983; Cuban, 1988). We also know that they are the least likely to engage students in more powerful learning experiences and that this kind of teaching supports a philosophical view of students as empty vessels waiting to be filled. It is hard to imagine that by helping teachers to hone those techniques, the educational experiences of the students would be made more powerful.

CHAPTER 5

MARY JONES
A Reflective Teacher Leader

A teacher leader is a person who can think and be creative with solutions. A person who has the guts to follow his/her own principles.

A teacher leader is a person who is recognized for having some expertise in the art of teaching and is able to share that with others—teachers, other professionals.
—Two of Mary's colleagues

THE CONTEXT

Mary Jones works in the Evergreen School District in the northwestern part of the United States. Her district is currently in the throes of transition from a wealthy, growing, suburban district to an urban district experiencing declining enrollments, the rapid growth of minority populations, and a graying teaching force. Fortunately, in light of the growing challenges, the district itself has had a long history of innovation and a reputation for exceptional education. At the time of this study, the district was in the third year of a major experimental project to shift decision making in schools from the central office to the school site. The administration and the union had forged some of the strongest contractual language for shared, site-based decision making in the country. As a result, each building was responsible for allocating resources for materials, staff development, and scheduling, and was experimenting with different kinds of decision-making bodies in order to reach "reasonable consensus"

101

within the staff. Each building was governed by a coordinating council of teachers, an administrator, and a parent or community member.

Another project, aimed at school improvement and begun 5 years before, involved teachers. In order to provide more leadership opportunities for teachers and to ensure that staffs had better building-based follow-up in a variety of curricular areas, the district had created a number of positions called "instructional support teachers" (ISTs). These positions were advertised district-wide for teachers and provided full-time release for an IST to work with faculty in a couple of buildings in the district. Selection of the ISTs was conducted by a committee of building-level and central office administrators. The IST then worked with two buildings throughout the school year to determine the specific building focus for school improvement. Essentially, the IST was available to teachers to coach them in new instructional programs, to conduct in-service workshops, to provide information and literature on current research, to do model lessons, and/or to run support groups of teachers who were interested in learning a particular skill or technique.

The district provided the ISTs with a good deal of training from national experts on new instructional techniques such as cooperative learning, critical thinking, Math Their Way, and writer's workshop. The model, then, was really to provide in-house experts to make training and follow-up available at the building level. The differences between Mary's and Gwen's positions were several in that ISTs here were assigned to two buildings rather than one and were on full-time release from the classroom. In addition, Mary was responsible for providing support for teachers in a variety of instructional techniques that covered various subject areas. Gwen's position concentrated on one theory of teaching that was not subject-matter specific. The ISTs in Mary's district were also provided with a collective office at the central administration building where they could meet as a group and work together as they mastered their various helping roles. These positions were considered prestigious and provided teachers with an inside track into administrative ranks. Many of the district principalships and assistant principalships were filled by ISTs.

During the year that this study was conducted, these roles were in a state of transition. As a result of the building-based decision making, one elementary staff had determined that they would rather disperse the money allocated for the IST among the entire staff. This idea gained popularity rapidly and, consequently, many of the ISTs were unsure as to whether their positions would be firm for much longer. Obviously, the circumstances were delicate for the ISTs; they were struggling to understand the rejection of their roles by the schools as part of the movement to participatory decision making rather than as a personal rejection. At the same time, few of them relished the notion of returning to the classroom full time because they loved the work they were doing.

Mary and her colleague, Barbara, were both ISTs at the middle-school level. They had held IST positions for 4 years and believed the positions to be problematic, even before the rejection of the IST position by the elementary school staff. As ISTs they had had difficulty getting into classrooms and finding meaningful ways to work with other teachers. They had to be invited.

> We often strategized over how to weasel our way into classrooms where help was needed. Administrators tended to let us in on where help was needed. Still we had to be invited—always on the premise that we were all good, but could all get better. It was very unstructured. We all felt unsuccessful and that we weren't contributing. We all established good relationships with other teachers, but they didn't think they were helped by us. They didn't buy into the position.

As a result, Mary and Barbara appealed to the district to allow them to change their positions a year before the IST positions came under fire. They had presented the SIP (the Shower Inspiration Project, so named because it had come to Barbara while she was in the shower) and had been able to create their own improved version of the IST position prior to the shake-up. Their proposal suggested an interdisciplinary, heterogeneous classroom demonstration center.

The two of them were engaged in team-teaching 57 sixth graders during four of the six periods of the day. Their students were heterogeneously mixed and reflected the minority populations within the school. Mary and Barbara believed that by returning to the classroom, they could put into action the many instructional strategies that they had been trying to teach. Other teachers could come in to watch, and they could model not only instructional innovation but the peer coaching they believed was so critical to teachers when learning new strategies. Thus, the idea was to create a demonstration site. The other two periods of the day were allocated for planning and for any of the more traditional requests for help from an IST. They conducted in-service in other buildings, served on the district-wide planning committee for a middle-school conference, worked on several projects with professors from the local university, and collaborated on writing a district-wide curriculum guide on interdisciplinary instruction. In addition, they had three student teachers who would be with them for 2 years. They worked in the north wing of the school in two classrooms that had a folding door between them, which could easily be moved for whole-group instruction. Their classroom location separated them from the rest of the school physically. In addition, the mere fact that they held IST positions, and that they had two planning periods at the same time every day, separated them from the rest of the teaching faculty. Both were paid regular teaching salaries.

The building administrators were receptive to the project, although Mary and Barbara had been told to play down their project with the rest of the staff. This directive bothered Barbara and Mary, and they had not been given satisfactory answers as to why they should behave in this way. Ostensibly, it was to reduce what the assistant principal called the "star syndrome." As a result, they said little about their program to other teachers, which had an ironic effect. Although the project was established as a demonstration center, people within the building knew little about it and so did not use it as a demonstration site. Thus, their redesigned teacher leadership role lacked people to lead.

The principal was new to the building this year, replacing a very proactive principal. Mark, by contrast, was more "laid back" and relaxed. He helped Barbara and Mary to obtain 16 computers with adequate wiring and believed they were doing important work. As of May, he had visited their classroom only once. Helen, the vice principal, was their evaluator and, as such, had more contact with them.

Their program is terrific and it's taken this year to stabilize the program, but it does not provide leadership for the rest of the staff. I have not worked hard to get other teachers scheduled in and they [Mary and Barbara] have not reached out. They aren't visible nor have they extended themselves in any way. I don't know why. There have been lots of university people here which has been a good connection, but it is not a good connection for this school. There are lots of hurt feelings.

Helen went on to say that she thought they could do a better job in the next year of incorporating the program into the staff, but that they needed to avoid the "star syndrome." She felt that their separateness came in part from the nature of their program, and that the staff felt the full spectrum of emotions from curiosity to jealousy. She had never communicated these concerns to Mary and Barbara.

A good deal of support came from the central office. The director for secondary education was very supportive of the program and met with Mary and Barbara frequently in order to check their progress. Another of the ISTs, Janice, who was on a part-time contract to do cooperative learning, also spent a good deal of time in their room. She had been in on the initial planning for the project and so was considered a partner in the endeavor. The director of curriculum also worked with the two women and provided them with extra contract days to write a first-round, interdisciplinary curriculum guide based on their experiences. In addition, numbers of school people from neighboring districts visited frequently so that the classroom felt very much like a lab within a larger, separate school.

While I was there, the program was encountering some resistance from the regular classroom teachers. The whole school was engaged in the process of scheduling for the next year. The demonstration program required a long block of time for students to work. In addition, since Mary and Barbara were trying to put into practice current beliefs about how best to educate students, they did not want students to leave for special pullout programs because they were experimenting with heterogeneity. The health education and arts teachers had asked that their programs be changed to pullout programs so that they would have the opportunity to work with smaller numbers of students. Mary and Barbara were opposed, whereas the rest of the sixth-grade staff were very enthusiastic, because it meant that they would have reduced student loads for a regular period of time several days a week. During the course of the discussion about whether this scheduling change should be put in place or not, parents were being consulted to check their reaction to the program changes. Mary and Barbara were hopeful that their parents would lobby strongly enough in their favor. The tension between the two camps of teachers was thick.

One final contextual factor is important. In the last few months of the school year, the first year of their experimentation, Barbara had applied for and received a year's leave of absence. A very strong, creative teacher, she felt that, after years of teaching, she needed to try something else, to break away to gain some perspective. She had no position lined up but was looking forward to the whole adventure. Mary, on the other hand, was grieving about Barbara's going, although supportive of her decision. Their close working relationship had been the basis for undertaking this experimental project; Mary was quite worried about whether she would be able to find another partner with whom she could work so well.

THE PERSON

Mary is one of those deceptively quiet people who, in a very short while, creates an imposing presence. When I entered her classroom for the first time, I felt an immediate sense of quiet, calm activity and warmth. Mary is a short, pretty woman with gray hair and snappy blue eyes. Her physical presence is quiet, but her eyes seem to defy any such thought by sending out sparks of humor, rage, delight, excitement, so that if outsiders and students are even the least bit observant, they can read Mary instantly. She dresses casually and conveys a sense of comfort and a strong sense of integrity—an upright person.

Mary has a master's degree and enough credits beyond for several doctorates. She has been teaching for 31 years, all but 3 of which have been in this school district. She taught for 2 years in Africa at an overseas school where the students were from 51 countries. She speaks fondly of those 2 years and notes that they changed her perspective on the world and made her want to share that understanding with her students. Mary loves children, not in any soft or idealized sense but out of a strong respect for their intelligence, their capabilities, their imaginativeness. In the entire time I observed her, I never heard her raise her voice or speak crossly to the children.

> I just can't do it. If I spend the day yelling at the kids, I go home in a foul mood. I'm unpleasant to everyone—even my dog—and it just isn't worth it. I do not believe in devaluing or ridiculing kids in any way, shape or form—even those four kids who've given us so much trouble. I have seen plenty of evidence of teachers who de-value kids and I simply don't think I could work in partnership under such circumstances. It's also the criteria which doesn't come up on selection criteria for teachers, nor does it show up in the ap-plications. It is the love of students that really worries me. How does one build an atmosphere of support for kids?

Mary works on a regular teacher's salary but has an extended contract to do the curriculum guide for the district during a couple of weeks in the summer. She is very reflective about the time she spent as a full-time IST. During the first couple of years, she and Barbara and Janice were assigned to the middle schools in order to help with the transition from junior highs to middle schools. All of them received excellent training about adolescents, creating a better transitional school from elementary schools to high schools, and developmental stages of learning from the leading experts in the country. Mary notes that several times the district provided roundtable sessions with these experts, and she and her colleagues realized that they were struggling with the same problems and were experimenting with the same solutions. "I think I feel the greatest gift of the last 4 years has been that association with these people in education. They have been real beneficial to me." During that time, they arranged and conducted in-service sessions, working with teachers, parents, and administrators to ensure a smooth transition. It was an exciting time. She and her colleagues designed a tutorial program in all the middle schools that they believe is exemplary. They have made several presentations at the annual National Middle School Association conferences.

After the transition to middle school, she was assigned as an IST to the building in which she currently teaches. In that role, she was provided training in a whole variety of instructional programs that served to broaden her own repertoire for helping teachers.

We had training in cooperative learning. We had training in group process. We had training in working with conflict resolution. We had training in working with learning styles—adults and kids. We had training in higher level thinking. We've attended classroom management conferences—I mean, we have attended conferences all around the state and across the country and have given presentations, you know. I feel like I have just been really, totally saturated by the school district, especially the first two years when they budgeted for staff development and they really used the money well, I thought.

Her reasons for orchestrating the transition are clear:

We didn't feel we were as effective as we could be when visiting other teachers' classrooms. We wanted our own rules. We were subject to the other teacher's management. I sometimes found classes where kids didn't have to listen. Teachers found it tough to disconnect from their own busy work—they did, however, discipline their kids. Sometimes teachers would leave while we were teaching even though the purpose of the demonstration had been very clear. This project was born out of our frustrations. We also wanted to model peer coaching. In all the time I was an IST, I constantly asked teachers for feedback, but in all that time, only two teachers asked for feedback from me.

She feels now that the program is totally inappropriate because it leaves the ISTs alienated from other teachers.

Mary noted repeatedly that she feels more stretched this year than she ever has—stretched in terms of trying so many new things, working in partnership with two university programs, working with Barbara so closely. According to Mary, the interaction with the students has been the most fulfilling, but the collaboration with Barbara has also been very powerful.

In project time [when all of the kids are working collaboratively on interdisciplinary units] I am not as tolerant as Barb. I'm not good with kids who are not on task. She's taught me that kids can do more than one thing and still be listening. I have problems with constructive activity and movement and noise, but I monitor a lot and watch to see that the kids get assistance. I have given up a lot of control working in a team. Everything I do has to do with the other team member. I've been able to give up a lot of things and I don't even miss them. I like this way a lot better because the burden of teaching is greatly reduced. And, there are moments which are superb and where everything goes just right and it all works and there's someone else in the room to share it with.

In explaining why this year was different, she said:

When I drive to work in the morning, I try to figure out what is different. Well, first of all, it's the experience—the more you do, hopefully, the more you get better. I think I know so much more about learning and about, you know, both sides of the brain and I just feel like I have had a lot of training that I am able to put to use in the classroom. I also feel high esteem—more than I have ever felt. I feel that I am truly a professional person and that I am what I want to be in my profession.

Considering all that Mary did during the year, she had an enormous capacity for work and spent long hours at it. She seldom left the school before 5 p.m., and as far as I could tell from the stacks of work that came back to the students each day, she was working most evenings and part of the weekend as well.

Despite her great personal commitment to what was going on in their experimental classroom, Mary indicated that the year was also proving quite frustrating. Her feelings about the rest of the staff were mixed in that she believed that there were some fine professionals in her building but some most unprofessional people as well. Mary herself has clearly defined values in terms of what it means to be a professional.

Over the last 3 years I have had a steady decrease in salary. Still I work evenings and weekends and I choose to do so because it is necessary in my profession. If I am committed to this line of work and if I care about the quality of my work, I simply must.

It is disappointing to her "that teachers here are unwilling to go any further than absolutely necessary. They constantly complain that unless the district is willing to pay, no work. I am sick of it after 4 years of listening to such talk." She notes that although many of the visitors to their classroom have been outsiders, few have been from within the building and that this has been discouraging for her and for Barbara. She feels that:

> I have invested enormous personal energy in nurturing these people and there is no exchange—no valuing, no respect. The principal asked me to work on the lunchroom conversation and on positive attitudes towards kids. I feel exhausted by that request. How is it possible to sit down in the midst of negativity during your break and change the tone?

A DAY WITH MARY

The school is tucked away on a dead-end street behind a series of apartment complexes—just off a major suburban thoroughfare. It is a pretty place, modern, well kept, tidy, with pleasant stands of fir trees surrounding the campus. Mary's room is off the north end of the school. The two rooms she and Barbara share open onto a large crushed-rock courtyard with a few benches. The two of them were given this location because the two rooms share a common space, which made it easy for them to monitor student break time. A folding wall can be pulled out of the interior walls to create two rooms for individual class work. Mary and Barbara share responsibility for 57 sixth-grade students. The children have been selected to represent a heterogeneous mix of ability levels, ethnicity, and gender. In addition, they have several students who are mainstreamed during their 4-hour block. Barbara and Mary teach math, language arts, science, social studies, and keyboarding, using an integrated approach to their curriculum. It is May, at the end of their first year in this experimental program.

Mary's day begins early as she and Barbara arrive an hour before school begins to attend a team meeting, which occurs once a month or more often if needed. Today's agenda involves planning the end-of-the-year field trip to the local zoo. People slowly drift into the classroom of one of the other sixth-grade teachers with coffee cups and plan books. There is light conversation. They begin by discussing who will be awarded the student-of-the-month awards. The discussion turns to sack lunches versus a barbecue for their field trip. The barbecue will involve parents, and there is a long pause as no one leaps to contact parents. One woman notes that she had a lousy time getting parents to cooperate last year. Someone else mentions that if they decide to do a barbecue, they will have to collect money. The entire tone of the meeting is directed toward organizing a trip that requires the least amount of work. Barbara steps in in an attempt to change the direction. She says she will organize the parents if someone else will help her. She gets a volunteer. They then discuss whether they should do worksheets for the bus ride or a scavenger hunt while at the zoo. Mary volunteers to show her safari slides from Africa for the entire sixth grade. She also says she will organize the activities they will carry out while at the zoo. Another teacher suggests a film about animals and says she will get it in. A 10-minute discussion follows on whether they should take the kids for a walk around a small lake near the zoo after lunch or bring them back to school. The team is clearly divided between those who want that opportunity for the kids and those who believe that too many of the students will misbehave. The issue is left unresolved, to be determined at their next meeting. The counselor asks that they hand in their placement forms on each student. After several other announcements, the team dismisses with no love lost. The atmosphere is chilly and formal. Mary is clearly angry at the other team members and mutters about their lack of professionalism and their disrespect for kids. She feels indignant that she and Barbara are always the champions of the kids and the ones who take charge of all of their collaborative ventures.

Mary and Barbara retreat to opposite corners of their room before the kids and the student teachers arrive so that they can breathe a moment of silence before the day begins. In the morning the doors between the two rooms are open so that the space seems large and quiet. The walls are tastefully decorated with a combination of trade posters and students' work. The students' work consists of posters demonstrating the concept of elaboration. There are comic faces with giant noses, flapping ears, huge bellies. There are examples of student writing. There are posters the kids did to represent themselves—T-shirt shapes covered over with pictures cut out from magazines, representing their interests. The trade posters reflect "You can do it" kinds of messages, self-esteem builders. Computer boxes are stacked nearly up to the ceiling in one corner. Both teachers have appealed to the district a number of times to get rid of them, but it seems that the bureaucracy moves slowly in the box-removal department. The counters around the room hold 16 computers, spread widely apart enough so that several students can cluster around each computer. Behind the computers are books, collections of paperbacks, reference books, and so forth.

At opposite ends of both rooms there are giant sectioned cupboards. Each student has a space in these closets to put coats, lunches, duffel bags. At rest, the cupboards look like fat connoisseurs of children's clothing—a red sweater drips from stuffed lips. In both rooms there are good-quality portable stereos with speakers and a pile of tapes ranging from classical music to heavy metal. Along one wall there are bookshelves filled with traditional textbooks that I never saw used during the course of my observations. The room is a lively, interesting place that expresses a kind of student-centeredness. As it filled up with children, I was readily aware that they felt quite at home here.

After comparing time schedules with Barbara, Mary pulls the wall shut. She begins the day by reviewing her lesson plans and by writing an introductory activity on the overhead that sits next to her desk in the front of the room. "Good Morning! Write: How dialogical reasoning (both sides) is different from my side reasoning. Which is better? Why? Write neatly and put your name on the paper. Thank you." She stands at the front of the room and greets the students in an unobtrusive way as they come in. She posts a list of what is due and who needs to do what. The children cram books into their desks, get snacks out, stuff their coats into the cupboard, and greet their friends. Several boys put a tape in and adjust the volume with one eye on Mary. Another little boy with an immaculate buzz haircut goes through his lunch and throws out anything that is healthful—a pear, yogurt—and keeps the potato chips and the cookies. Several little girls compare outfits and hairdos. One little girl has a long French braid and bangs glued with hairspray into an elaborate swirl. The others are clearly envious. Most of the boys have haircuts that require moussed spikes or hairspray to make the hair stand on end. They have on brightly colored tennis shoes that look to weigh 10 pounds apiece. None of them have the shoes laced up, and it seems to be important that the tongue of the tennis shoes stick out. I do not remember sixth graders being so interested in fashion and am a bit dazzled by the color and array. The sixth graders in Gwen's school were dressed more conservatively. I wondered whether it was reflective of the socioeconomic levels of the two communities or the difference between middle school and grade school students.

Gradually, the children sit down and begin to write. The room grows quiet. After 10 minutes of their writing, Mary says good morning and asks them to share their papers with a neighbor and to add anything into their own work that they did not think of or that they forgot. After a few minutes of quiet conversation, she asks that they hand the papers in and that they share their answers. Several children explain dialogical reasoning. Next she asks them to think about the field trip to an exhibit called Body Works, which had demonstrated how the body works through all kinds of machines, exercise equipment, and slides. One girl explains the purpose of the exhibit. Another student describes what he thought was most cool. Several others offer their opinions. Mary echoes their likes and moves them to demonstrate the diversity of their preferences, "So you liked the electromagnetic body. How about something else that one of you liked the best?"

Mary switches gears by asking them to close their eyes and empty their brains so that they can get ready for something new. She speaks to the students in a very quiet voice. As a result, the students are very quiet so that they can hear. They close their eyes and again there is a brief period of silence. She notes that they will now move into their immigrant unit and that she needs to collect their timelines and to give them another project before allowing them project time. As they hand in their timelines, a historical documentation of the Irish immigration to the United States, she asks them where they had difficulty with the assignment. They make a few comments, but do not appear to have found the assignment difficult. She then assigns a family tree, asking them to take out their "immigrant" booklets, which she and Barbara have created for this unit. Someone reminds her that she has not handed them out yet and volunteers. Mary grins, says she is getting senile, and thanks the student. As the students get their packets, they ask questions about the family tree. "What if our grandparents are dead?" "How far back should we go?" "What about maiden names?" "What if we don't know how to spell some of their names?" "Yeah, what if some of the names are in foreign languages like my grandma? I only know how to write her name in Persian." She answers all the questions, noting after each one, "What a good question" or "I'm glad you asked that" or "I hadn't thought of that." Once the questions are finished, she reminds them about their journal work, their LOGO assignments, their math work, and tells them that they will have the next 45 minutes before break as project time. She reminds them that the trees outside the classroom have been sprayed with some toxic chemical and that during break, they should avoid climbing on them. Two boys push the wall back and all 57 of them move.

The two groups of children quickly mix and pair off into groups of two and three or four. Several groups race to the computers to make sure that they get on right away. One little girl who looks like a new birch sapling sits down to read her novel, *Sweet Valley High*. She is immediately engrossed and seems oblivious to the noise around her. She does not move for the entire project period. An interracial group—two blacks, an Asian, and one white boy—push four desks together and proceed to work on their math. One of the boys goes to the cutter and slices paper into fractional segments for them to use. As they begin to work, they sing "I'm a Little Teapot" and laugh while doing the motions. Total lack of inhibition. Another tiny girl with long brown braids works with a tall Asian girl to get their computer partner, Mike, to work with them. Kittie has obtained a computer and is insistent that he come and help. He ignores them, until her persistence wears him down. "All right! Get me a pencil!" he shouts at her. Kittie puts her hands on her hips, leans her upper body forward, and shouts back in a smaller, squeakier, but equally firm voice, "I don't have to!" Mike grins, gets up, and moves with them to the computer. Kittie cheerfully rattles off what they have to do.

Two other boys work on a computer together, trying to figure out the LOGO exercises in the package that Barbara has prepared for them. One leans into the computer from the right while the other sits on the back of his chair with his feet on the seat so that he can be at eye level with the computer. They carry on a lengthy discussion that consists of one-syllable words, eyes constantly on the computer screen as they attempt to make a circle and then chart their movements. "Try this." "Huh?" "Oh, no." "That's wrong." "Try this." "Wow!"

Three other kids begin working on their immigrant package. Again, it involves using a data base on the computer. The three of them huddle and read through the directions and piece together how they are to do this part of their assignment. They inform and correct each other with ease. Their responsibility is to adopt a character who will immigrate to the United States from Ireland. The boy in the group looks at the list of possibilities and says, "What's a farm man do?" These are clearly city kids. No one in their group knows, so they ask Mary as she passes by. She laughs and says, "Haven't any of you kids been on a farm?" Because they have not, she says she should organize an excursion and then tells them about farm work. They decide their immigrant will not be a farmer because he will not have enough money to get started in the United States.

Another group of students gathers around another woman who has come in without my noticing. They are working on reading right in the middle of everyone else, and seem able to concentrate. Another smaller group of students works with one of the student teachers who looks just like Annette Funicello, flip and all. She is going over their math assignments with them, working on fractions and decimals. Barbara and Mary wander from group to group answering questions and helping groups of students to focus. The boy with the buzz haircut checks to see where the teachers are and dashes out the door. No one notices. Another large, blond boy moves from group to group pinching and punching in a generally disruptive fashion. Mary attempts to get him working on something at his desk. The room hums with activity.

At this point, the door opens and seven teachers and a central office administrator from a neighboring school district come in. They have contacted Mary and Barbara because they are interested in interdisciplinary learning. Teachers in their school already work in teams of four. However, each of the teams has tended to divide up the labor—one taking responsibility for English, one for Math—rather than integrating the curriculum. Mary moves to greet them while Barbara continues to circulate and work with the students. Mary and Barbara alternate playing the host to visiting groups. They ask Mary several questions. She explains what is going on and then tells them to look around for a few minutes, after which she will answer any questions they might have. She says that the students are used to having adults in the room and will also be happy to answer their questions. This group, too, fans out and moves to observe various groups of students.

The door opens again, and a young man with a video camera comes in. He checks in with Barbara and then begins to tape several groups of students who are working on computers. Mary sees Ken, the student who left the room, come in. She slowly makes her way over to him and asks where he's been. He says he's gone down to see the counselor, but that the counselor was busy and so he's made an appointment for later. Mary reminds him that it is not okay to leave the room like that. He acknowledges his error and then stomps away, swearing just within my earshot.

One of the students, Haten, asks me for some help with his family tree. It is apparent that any adult in the room is fair game for help. He tells me that his family escaped from Iran just before the Shah was overthrown. His father was a TV announcer in Iran. They have been here for 9 years and own a dry-cleaning business. They have some other relatives here. They speak Farsi at home, and his mom would go back in a flash if they could, but he does not remember it very well. He understands all about being an immigrant though, because he and his brother had to learn English and then teach their parents. He has on turquoise, unlaced, high-top tennis shoes, green-and-white-striped socks, huge baggy jams with every color in the rainbow, a blue-and-white-striped T-shirt, different from either his shoes or his shorts. He has a giant Swatch watch in other colors still—a veritable sheikh of color. He moves away to work on his LOGO assignment, saying that he must get Barbara to help him because he is not so good with this stuff. As I watch him walk away, I notice that very few of the students are sitting at desks. They sprawl on the desks or sit on the floor or stand over their desks. Only five students in the whole room are sitting at their desks.

After about 20 minutes of observing in different parts of the room, the visiting teachers gather back in around Mary. While the students continue to work, she answers the rapid-fire questions they have. "How do you use the computers and who schedules the students on them?" Mary says that they assign partners in some cases— usually on the computers because they like to make sure that at least one student is competent in computer skills. Then the students cooperate in determining who will use the computers when. During project time, the students are free to work on any of the assignments that they need to complete and so, somehow, it all seems to work out all right. They ask a variety of questions about scheduling. Mary makes it clear that in order to conduct this experiment, she and Barbara gave up their duty-free recess time, which causes the visitors to lapse into momentary silence. They do not feel that their group would be willing to do this. They ask about the absence of bells, about evaluation of the kids' work, about whether the kids are learning more this way than in regular classroom instruction. Mary notes that the comprehensive type of evaluation they had counted on had not been developed, but that she and Barbara are working in partnership with several professors at the university to see how the students are responding to integrative instruction. Both teachers currently believe that math anxiety is greatly reduced because "students don't even know they're doing math."

She notes that because they do not allow any students to be pulled out of the classroom, and because all of the students are working in groups anyway, there is less awareness about learning deficiencies, which is better for those students' self-esteem. The visitors ask for a description of a typical day, and Mary describes when and why she and Barbara close the door and how long they do project time. The visiting teachers ask about integrated units and where curricular materials are obtained. Mary says, "We make up a good deal of it because good materials just don't exist." She pauses to help Tim, a recent immigrant student, and then comments that it is easier for elementary-trained teachers to do this because they are more used to integrating curriculum than are secondary teachers. Another teacher asks how the parents are responding to the program. Mary passes out copies of *Cider Press*, the newsletter for parents she and Barbara put together about the work they are doing. In the newsletter they explain what the students are working on and how parents might be helpful. They have also included articles on the intellectual and emotional development of sixth-grade students and research on learning. They include a tear-off sheet for comments from the parents and have received a good deal of positive response. Several of the parents have called to see if the same program will be available for their students the next year, and Mary says, "All we can say is that it's being talked about but we don't know." The questioning goes on for several minutes more. The visitors are most appreciative as they leave, asking if they can send another group of their colleagues the next week. Mary says it is fine as she turns back to the classroom to get ready for recess.

She and Barbara use loud voices to call the students back to their own seats in order to clean up before break time. The children move quickly; they leap over chairs, jump, twist, and slide into their seats. Few of them walk. Once the room is reassembled and quiet, Mary and Barbara give their respective classes directions to switch rooms when they come back from break and then dismiss them. Some students roar outside while others congregate in different parts of the room. Several girls sit around a couple of desks to make colored-pencil peelings. The peelings look a little like flowers; they concentrate and put them carefully on pieces of paper to decorate the top of their desks. Another group of boys sits on the floor in Barbara's room with the stereo up as loud as is permissible. They sing along, "I don't give a good Goddamn . . . ," just out of earshot and look very pleased. This is the gang of four. One is the victim of severe abuse by his alcoholic father, who is no longer around. Two others are also from single-parent homes, living with their mothers. One of these is in a very destructive stage and responds to nothing that Mary and Barbara have tried to do for him. The fourth, with the buzz haircut, comes from a family who buys him everything. Currently, his father has told him that if he is good in school for the remainder of the year he will get a jet ski for the summer. Mary and Barbara have worked individual contracts with the four boys, and spend a good deal of their time trying to keep track of these boys and to engage them in some kind of productive work. At this point, feeling almost dry of ways to help the boys, the two teachers frequently discuss how much time they should devote to police these four and how much time they should devote to helping the others who are willing and happy to learn.

Two other boys are collecting Swatches—plastic watches—from their friends. One has collected 12 and has them all on his arm. Another group of girls is clustered around the other stereo. A boy approaches and one of them says, "Your epidermis is showing!" He turns scarlet and immediately checks his zipper. Then he looks confused and checks out several other possibilities as he races outside. The girls are giggling hysterically. Sixth-grade humor!

During break, Barbara and Mary regroup, assessing how project time went, whether the visitors disrupted the students' time, whether the videotaping went all right. Last week they had a number of visitors from Canada. They compare questions, because Barbara worked with the last group. Mary notes that one of the student teachers will be doing a 30-minute poetry lesson with Barbara's students while they are with Mary for English during the next period. Mary needs 1 hour together with all of them, and then another project time is agreed upon. Barbara will work with Mary's students on math and on the new Logo activities. They open the doors and call the students back in.

Once in their seats, the students are asked by Mary to close their eyes and think of the quietest, calmest place they have ever been. She asks them to visualize that place and to feel the quietness for a few minutes so that they can clear their minds. The room is silent, peaceful. She then reviews what they will be doing for the next 2 hours before lunch. The student teacher takes over to conduct a lesson on personification. She explains personification as giving things life. They have a tentative discussion about the literary device and about poetry and why we have to study it. The discussion is labored. She has difficulty responding to their comments and holding her next steps in mind. Mary sits in the back of the room taking notes and observing while the student teacher's university supervisor sits in the corner in the front of the room taking notes as well. Mary notes that the observation form used by the university faculty is a long checklist, and that, because it is so demanding, the supervisor never looks up to see what the students are doing. She also tells me that her approach to working with student teachers is to explain her personal philosophy of working with children. She describes her rationale for approaching any curricular issue with the student teachers while she communicates to them that there are a variety of ways of doing things. She tries to avoid right/wrong discussions with them. She wants to create a working relationship that encourages their ideas. The student teacher gives the students an assignment and they groan. She negotiates by saying, "I know it's another rotten assignment. You do not have to do a rough draft or a final draft—but please write neatly." By the end of the 30 minutes the student teacher looks completely spent and slides into the corner to discuss the lesson with her supervisor. Mary moves back to the class, gives them the same assignment she gave the earlier group, and dismisses them for another project time.

Three students gather around another computer and explain to me that they are attempting to get their pilot's licenses, which means that they learn to work the various components of APPLEWORKS. When they have completed the assignment, they are able to teach it to other students; hence the pilot's license. Janice, the IST who specializes in cooperative learning, comes into the room to observe. She spends a fair bit of her time coaching Barbara and Mary on their use of cooperative groups. Janice visits with students and observes quietly from different vantage points in the room. Mary and Barbara are both busy roaming the room, answering questions and helping students to solve problems. One of the boys shows me a magazine he is reading titled *Irish American*. He too understands what it is to be an immigrant because his mother is Turkish, his father Italian. This is the third country in which he has lived in his short life. He speaks three languages fluently and is also teaching his mother to speak English. He shows me an excerpt written by Richard Harris in the magazine: "There comes a time in your life when you have to exercise your own belief; and you only get that through going through life, by experiencing life, by actually running the length of your wildness and discovering what kind of solace or fulfillment that gave you" (*Irish American*, April 1988, p. 37). Luigi checks some of the words but gets the gist of it. He reckons that he has had a lot of experiences.

This project time is spent in much the same way as the earlier session. There is a busy hum in the room. Students continue to work and seem engaged and busy. The atmosphere in the classroom is, however, very different from a traditional classroom where everyone is seated at individual desks while the whole group engages in the same activity. Because of the integrated nature of the program, there is no set time for math, for English, for social studies. The students are doing this work in the midst of the immigrant unit, and they choose which aspect of the unit they wish to work on during project time with their friends. As a result, the classroom looks more like a summer camp workshop than a traditional classroom. Several students choose to work alone; a few others seem to work at avoiding work—they watch the teachers and circulate out of their field of vision. At first glance, it is difficult to know with any certainty whether the students are working or goofing off. In many cases, there is laughter and a sense of camaraderie. Hours of observation led me to believe that the students were engaged in their work and spending their time productively with a minimum of boredom and struggle.

Several minutes before lunchtime, the students are asked to return to their seats. Mary stands in the center of the room and, using an overhead, asks all of the students to concentrate for a few minutes on how they used project time. She then asks them to write down what they did and to evaluate on paper whether they believe that they used their time well. Finally, she asks them to indicate whether she and Barbara could have done anything to help them use that time more efficiently. They write quietly for 7 minutes. She then reminds them of due dates, has them turn in their papers, tidy the room, put their chairs up, and dismisses them for lunch. She and Barbara stand by their respective doors to say good-bye. The sudden quiet in the empty room is quite shocking.

The student teacher (whose supervisor has left), Barbara, Janice, Mary, and I troop down to the faculty room, which is complete with a phone, a lunchcounter window into the kitchen, soda machines, and a microwave. One wall is all glass and looks out onto a small private courtyard where several smokers have congregated. We sit at a round table by ourselves. Although the room is relatively full, there is no exchange; people continue to eat and visit in their own groups. Our conversation centers around the boy who has been abused by his father. Barbara and Janice discuss whether he might not be suicidal, whether they should contact his mother, how a coming presentation by a state agency on child abuse will affect him. Mary, disturbed by one of the teachers who is talking loudly at the next table, notes quietly that, given the choice, they would eat at the central office. "The company's much better." The conversation ranges over the development of curriculum for the kind of teaching they are doing, their constant worry as to whether students are using their time well, and how much education has changed in the course of Mary's career. "Even though I have been running as fast as I can, it's difficult to keep up with what's coming in education. I've been teaching since 1957 and there have been so many changes—television, telecommunications, space travel, etc." She struggles just to try to keep up with the computers. She and Barbara laugh and explain that really their collaboration has caused Mary to leap into the computer world. The student teacher listens with great interest and notes that things have certainly changed since she was last in school.

After lunch, Janice and Barbara debrief for 5 minutes. They count the number of responses they received on the last newsletter and review the names of those parents they need to contact for a variety of reasons. They discuss silent reading time and the new drug and alcohol curriculum they want to cover. Barbara takes responsibility for getting that organized. They check their timeline on the interdisciplinary curriculum, and Mary agrees to make several phone calls and to do some writing. They check their calendar for next week's visitors, for the two in-services they are planning, and for a lesson that another IST will do on listening skills. They agree to review again first thing in the morning and convene a discussion with the three student teachers who have wandered into the room. They debrief the lessons taught by two of the student teachers in the last 2 days. The two teachers conduct the discussion by asking questions about how the student teachers felt, whether their purposes were met, what they believed was the strongest part of the lesson. The discussion moves to the teaching of writing, and the student teachers question how Barbara and Mary teach spelling. They explain that their experience and research confirm that direct instruction of spelling does not work particularly well and that they now focus on teaching the students dictionary skills, proofreading, and peer editing as a means to ensure that final products are in good shape. The student teachers argue, based on the philosophy of their methods professor at the university. One says, "The major weakness of this program is the kids' decoding skills. They are simply not getting enough work in this area." It is clear that university professors hold more credibility than the collective experience of the cooperating teachers. Barbara and Mary listen respectfully and note that there are many different opinions about the teaching of spelling and that the student teachers will have to formulate their own. They reinforce their reasons in a nondefensive discussion.

At this point, the door opens again and a professor from the university, with whom they are working on the evaluation of their program, comes in with the director of secondary education from the district central office and Janice, the other IST. The entire group pushes another table into place and the conversation expands and shifts. They have convened to discuss the final steps of the experimental design of their evaluation program and to plan an end-of-the-year retreat to analyze and assess the efficacy of the program. Another professor who is an expert on integrative learning will join them for that analysis. Mary notes that she is still angry because no one else in the school would agree to function as the control group; she just cannot understand it. In the course of their conversation, they establish the posttest dates and procedures, determine that they will wear disreputable clothes at the retreat, and swap many funny stories about language and idioms and students. Finally, Ann, the professor, announces that she has just agreed to take a position in another part of the country. Everyone is extremely disappointed, because each has really relied on her to help figure out ways in which to check on the viability of their program. At the same time, they are happy for her as she dips into the southern accent indicative of the place where she is going and where she grew up. Ann suggests that Barbara, because she is looking for a change of venue, might wish to consider teaching the classes at the university, an unusual sign of respect. Barbara declines but is appreciative. They all wonder who will help to design and conduct any kind of study next year. As the meeting concludes and the visitors disappear, both Barbara and Mary indicate what a privilege it has been to work with these people, even though they had originally thought the professors would spend far more time in their classrooms than they actually did. Originally they had been told that one-fourth of their time would be spent here. As it turned out, their visits were infrequent. Still, it had been a rewarding exchange.

Very shortly, the two of them fling books, files of papers, and computer disks into big baskets, turn out the lights, and race out the door to a meeting at the central office. Their purpose at this meeting is to recap the year for their fellow ISTs and discuss their feelings about the experimental project. As they race up the stairs, the two women outline what they will cover and how. They wish they had more time to prepare.

There are 17 people gathered around a big table. Everyone is friendly and interested. This also is the IST group whose jobs are under consideration at the moment, so they are particularly attentive to the alternatives Barbara and Mary have created. Barbara begins by asking the group to write for a few minutes about the difference between interdisciplinary and integrated curriculum. The room is quiet for a few minutes, and the leaders discuss the various distinctions between the two. Janice notes that this is one of the differences they have been led to consider as central to their philosophy by one of the professors with whom they are working. She describes how the original proposal changed because of the reality of having to exist within the rigid structure of a school timetable. Barbara and Mary describe what a typical day is like, where the challenges lie, and where they feel that they have been most successful. The constant search for curriculum and the consequent constant need to create it has been extremely problematic. Several other ISTs in the room give their assessment of the program as a most powerful mode teaching and leading. Both Barbara and Mary discuss the importance of their partnership and of Janice's coaching. Their work together made all of the uncertainty and all of the challenge more "do-able."

At this point the conversation changes to the implications of this kind of instruction. The discussion is deep and thoughtful. Several of the participants claim that they clearly do not want to go back into the classroom to do this kind of work. Mary concludes by summing up what caused her personally to make the shift and to push herself so hard: "If you value students to the very highest level of your being, then you have to behave in these ways, you have to try to find new ways that work." It is close to 5:30 when the group disperses. Mary and Barbara hurry off to their cars to go home to eat, to plan for the next day, and to review student work.

OTHER RESPONSIBILITIES

Mary's days were typically this full and occasionally more so. I observed her in meetings with principals to organize in-service or special projects in the various schools where she had been an in-service specialist. One afternoon, she conducted a 3-hour in-service session for fellow middle school teachers on the teaching of writing. She worked with adults in much the same way that she did with children—functioning as a facilitator of their expertise, valuing their particular experiences—while adding information from current research on writing and working them through new techniques with which they were not familiar.

Another afternoon I observed her as she participated in a first-time experience, the selection of her new team partner. Because of Mary's very strong feelings about professionalism and her attitudes toward valuing students, she was very anxious that her new partner be someone with whom she could work well. The position had been opened and a number of people she knew had applied. She felt that she simply could not sustain the energy required for such extensive experimentation unless she worked with someone who had similar values. Her anxiety came from years of experience in the district and and her belief that teachers did not have the proper kind of authority to influence decisions in these processes. During the course of that meeting, she clarified the purposes of the program and the values they wished to communicate to fellow staff members and students for the principal and the director of secondary education. She also made it very clear that the selection of an appropriate partner was essential to her continuing participation. The administrators responded to her criteria by generating a rating scale that gave weight to her requirements—clearly a sign of their respect for her.

In addition, she constantly built time for the student teachers so that she could give them the kind of support she believed was most helpful to them. In one instance, one of the student teachers had conducted an excellent lesson on acculturation but felt it was a failure. During the course of the lesson, she admitted failure to the students. During the debriefing session, Mary suggested to her that she and Barbara work very hard to get students out of the failure syndrome and that they want to communicate to students that experimentation is okay. She then suggested other ways the student teacher might have concluded the lesson without modeling her concerns about failure. Mary notes in private that this particular student teacher is in need of a great deal of support, as she is getting a divorce, buying a house, single parenting, taking 20 credits, and trying to do this month-long intensive observation. She is very insecure and uptight, and intervenes in negative ways when Mary and Barbara are dealing with students. In order to cope with this situation, Mary and Barbara brainstormed ways to communicate their concerns to her in a positive way.

Barbara and Mary also spent several sessions with other teachers in order to discuss the scheduling issue for the coming year. In those meetings, facilitated by the counselor, each party stated his or her position. As is apt to happen in a place where people are unused to the processes of negotiation or mutual problem solving, they just kept repeating their opposite viewpoints as if continued dialogue of this nature would cause one of them to switch sides, which of course it did not. Feelings simply ran deeper and deeper. During the course of these adversarial sessions, the parents determined that the schedule would not be changed for the next year. Still, even though Mary had another year to work the program as it existed, she was resentful of the other teachers' lack of consideration for the kind of work she was trying to do. The other teachers were equally resentful, believing that Mary and Barbara had enough special treatment.

In addition, Mary and Barbara spent a good deal of their time generating curricula that would support integrative learning. They spent long hours discussing the concepts they wished to convey, the subject matter that would allow them to get across those concepts, and the learning activities that would allow the students to gain firsthand, participatory understanding. Because so very little of this kind of material exists, they were constantly creating as they went—critiquing, and revising, and asking the students to critique. Both of them spent a significant amount of time in the evenings generating this material. Again, Mary's position required a good deal more of her than the contractual agreement. During the course of my observations, I never heard her complain about the demands of her job; I did hear her complain about the fact that there were not more hours in the day.

HER COLLEAGUES

During the course of my observations in Mary's school, I interviewed three of her colleagues: her partner, Barbara, who was the strong supporter; a fellow teacher whom Mary respected a good deal; and someone Mary did not believe was supportive. The union representative was not available for interviewing as she could not find the time. Mary's perceptions of the three that I did interview were accurate.

In all three cases, teachers at Mary's school indicated that there should be more leadership positions for teachers to reduce the isolation of teaching. In two cases, they believed that candidates for the positions should be selected by administrators because they have more knowledge of different teachers' competencies. The third colleague believed that teachers should select those who would be working with them. The three described a variety of positions that would help improve their own instruction and would have the potential to improve the quality of the teaching career. Suggestions ranged from positions where candidates could generate more creative, integrative lesson plans, to peer coaches, to quarter-long sabbaticals for planning. One of the interviewees suggested the kind of leadership density model mentioned earlier. She believed that several people should be selected to fulfill a variety of roles from scheduling to curriculum planning. Most important, however, she believed that teachers needed to be given adequate time to assume new responsibilities and adequate compensation.

Not surprisingly, Barbara considered Mary to be the very best kind of leader. She had worked closely with her for 8 years and believed that Mary's finest strengths lay in her ability to keep groups working on a positive track and to parry disagreements, turning them into productive discussions. She was willing to innovate and to risk. In fact, all of the interviewees agreed that Mary was a strong leader in that she was creative, industrious, caring, and knowledgeable. Barbara noted that the experimental project as they had originally conceived it was much bigger and more complex than what they were actually doing now, but the interdisciplinary teaching was much more difficult and time consuming than they had anticipated. As a result, they had not been able to provide the kind of assistance to other teachers they had anticipated.

The other two teachers felt that the current position did not provide leadership for them in particular. Although both recognized that Mary was involved in developing interdisciplinary teaching, neither of them had any clue as to how that was going. One in particular felt quite resentful.

> She doesn't function as a leader this year. She and Barb lead each other. As an IST, she was visible in that she gave classes in meetings or we'd hear about what they were doing. This year we just see each other in team meetings. I feel disappointment. I feel that they were supposed to share with us and they haven't. I'm really disappointed; I feel ripped off. I asked a number of times to come in and was put off. I couldn't tell what was going on. Then I see all the computers and the fancy equipment, the rest of us get damned jealous. The communication is not good at all. We don't know how they're doing their different subjects. It makes all of us mad. We were told that they would make presentations and they

haven't. If we don't know what goes on in there they haven't done their work well. We don't know where the computers have come from. Janice has spent all of her time with them. We'd like to see her here, too. The rest of us feel like lost children—as if we're just ignored. They are positive people and have added a calming influ-ence to our team. They're very helpful. Still, I don't have one iota of proof that their program is working, or even what they're doing in there. I observed because interdisicplinary teaching is one of my goals, but it took me a long time to get in. I think they're both good teachers, although I couldn't tell while I was in there what they were doing at all.

All of Mary's colleagues recognized that Mary had created the position she currently held. One of the women noted that the IST positions were dying because the parents and community were call-ing for fewer of these kinds of jobs. Although I had no indication that the disintegration of these positions came from anywhere but the individual school sites, these conversations clearly revealed that everyone understood that Mary's position was different from what it had been previously, and that it was moving toward providing leader-ship in a different way. Although Barbara indicated that the first year of their new project was far more difficult than they had anticipated, the other two teachers interviewed were not clear as to how that leadership would affect them. The fact that the administration had attempted to keep the program fairly quiet contributed to the confu-sion here.

THE CHARACTERISTICS OF TEACHER LEADERSHIP IN A DEMONSTRATION CENTER

Although the purpose of Mary's role is similar to both Ted's and Gwen's, the other general characteristics are quite different. The purpose of Mary's role is to promote instructional improvement for the teachers in her building. The model in which Mary worked might be called teacher leadership through demonstration. The incentives for taking the role are high for Mary; the role has provided her with great opportunities to learn and the freedom to experiment. The incentives to participate are not apparent for other teachers in the building. They must find the time to visit the demonstration classroom, and then must figure some way to make the experiences seen there meaningful and/or translatable to their own setting.

The effects of the role on the kids in Mary's classroom seemed, at first blush, to be positive. Students were engaged in an interdisciplinary learning experience in which they covered a number of subject areas. Their skills in basic subjects were equal to those of students in regular classrooms, and they were gaining computer literacy skills. At the same time, Mary, Barbara, and several of their evaluators believed that students had a more positive attitude toward learning. Because Mary and Barbara had not yet affected the teaching practices of other teachers in the school, the effects did not extend beyond their own students.

Mary's position did pose some significant challenges to the existing system. Because she and Barbara wished to team, they needed a room that could accommodate both whole-group and small-group instruction. Because they were experimenting with mainstreaming and with the elimination of pullout programs, specialists had to visit their classroom during their block period. Mary and Barbara had to agree to supervise their students during recess, usually a duty-free time for teachers. In addition, Mary and Barbara had to be willing to put in the time to develop their own curriculum because they had rejected standardized texts. Elective subjects—like band, choir, physical education, and languages—had to be offered in the afternoon so that their students could participate in these. Thus, the master schedule of the rest of the sixth grade teachers was affected. Mary and Barbara ostensibly lowered student loads by returning to the classroom to work with their 57 students. As was evident in the struggles over the specialist schedules for the next year, Mary and Barbara's program had a significant impact on the other teachers in the building.

The assumptions that undergirded Mary's role might look something like this:

1. Learning occurs through experimentation, collaboration, and reflection for both adults and students.
2. Experienced teacher leaders are able to reshape their own roles in order to promote better instruction; teachers can improve on a model developed by administrators.

3. Two teachers in a classroom are better than one.
4. When teacher leaders demonstrate different modes of instruction for their colleagues, the demonstration influences and improves the teaching skills of others.
5. In order to model improved instruction, teacher leaders need their own classroom to establish routines with children and to free visiting teachers to be learners instead of teachers.
6. Demonstration teachers need extra planning time and additional resources in order to be able to demonstrate a variety of instructional techniques.
7. Teacher leaders, after administrators, know best what teachers need to build improved instruction.
8. Instructional innovations, experimentation, and reflective practice are valued by the district.
9. Teacher leaders are curriculum developers.
10. Open communication about the demonstration center or the provision of time for teachers to visit would not improve its efficacy.

Although a number of these assumptions are positive, a number are problematic.

Mary's job involved two kinds of collaborative work. Mary and Barbara worked as partners. Barbara clearly believed that she gained a good deal from working with Mary. Two talented teachers shared responsibility for students, for curriculum, and for the development and refinement of their instructional program. In fact, both Barbara and Mary spoke frequently of what each gained personally from collaboration with the other. Barbara, for instance, gained skill in working with groups of adults and students in a more positive way as well as expertise on writing instruction. Mary, on the other hand, learned that children can actually do more than one thing at a time, and that they can learn in the midst of noise and movement. Barbara also taught Mary about computers and their integration into course work. Both believed that their own teaching improved as a direct result of their collaboration. Both felt strongly that the children were introduced to better curriculum and instruction as a result of their working together. Meaningful collaboration for these two teachers consisted of an equal relationship instead of the teacher/

student model of collaboration they were trying to put into place for other teachers. This collaboration seemed to be more in keeping with that suggested in Little's (1986) and Rosenholtz's (1989) work.

The colleagues with whom I spoke were less certain about the positive effects of collaboration with an IST. The old IST role was established with a different form of collaboration in mind—more like a mentoring role, where one teacher had expertise that he or she wished to impart to the other. Classroom teachers were uncertain about this relationship and had let Mary and Barbara know that they were troubled by it. They felt that if they invited the IST into their room, it was a kind of admission of weakness, of inability to handle their own classroom. The notion that everyone was a good educator, but could get better, had not really permeated the belief systems of the teachers. The new form of collaboration as conceived and implemented by Mary and Barbara in the demonstration center again focused on mentoring. The general reaction of the teachers was that it did little to affect them. The various attitudes toward opportunities to collaborate—in mentoring and partnering—suggest that consideration needs to be given to the form of collaboration.

DOMINANT THEMES

A number of themes emerged as I studied Mary's case. She and Barbara had a perception of their role different from that of the other teachers in the building. More striking, the two of them had redesigned their original IST position based on their own critique of their work, but had created a model burdened with its own set of problems.

Contrasting Metaphors

Perceptions play an important part in the understanding of a place and of relationships. Not surprisingly, Mary and her colleagues used dramatically different metaphors to describe the new IST role. Mary saw herself and Barbara as great explorers in the midst of a rich and fertile land where everyone else was blind to the wealth of opportunities surrounding them. She felt enormous frustration—if only the other teachers would agree to venture out a little. On the other hand, at least some of the rest of the staff appeared to perceive the situation in more feudal terms, pun notwithstanding. Mary and Barbara's classroom appeared to be the castle set apart from the huts of peasants. Important visitors flowed in and out on a regular basis, never visiting elsewhere. Resources also flowed in on a grand scale—16 computers and new and interesting software!—and, yet, these were two teachers just like everyone else. A confusing circumstance for the peasants.

Because the groups did not communicate well, their perceptions were unspoken but lay heavy in the air. Conversations between the two groups were restricted. Interactions were limited to only those that were necessary. No attempt had been made by either party to air perceptions or to clarify opposing views. As a result, the tension was high.

Reflective Practice and the Evaluation of Teacher Leadership

Perhaps the most unusual aspect of the creation of this new position was that it originated in Mary and Barbara's evaluation of their own work. In the course of their working together as ISTs, Janice, Barbara, and Mary sensed the poor construction of these positions almost a year before the unrest actually became more visible in the rest of the district. The fact that they spent considerable time uncovering reasons why their positions were not working demonstrates a kind of honest, reflective assessment that, at least in my experience in schools, is not typical. Nor is this kind of assessment characteristic of the kinds of formal teacher leadership positions I have observed.

Formal evaluations for both Mary's job and Gwen's job were conducted by the principal in much the same way that regular teacher evaluations are done. They met with the principal at the beginning of the year, set goals, and met again at the end of the year to determine whether they had met the goals. In no case did Mary's evaluation indicate that she needed to rethink the role. It is quite unusual that the teacher leaders themselves, given that their roles had been sanctioned by the administration, engaged in a serious critique of their own performance that caused them to redesign the role.

Professional Responsibility, Time, and Contractual Arrangements

Mary frequently railed against the traditional union stance—no more pay/no more work—which she heard from some of the teachers with whom she worked. Her belief was that she was a professional and, as such, had a professional responsibility to put in as much time as was necessary for her to do her very best. Mary represents the historical "teaching as a profession" argument, in that she believes that teachers must do everything in their power to better serve their clients—the students. She also represents a burgeoning number of teachers who would like opportunities to grow during the course of their professional lives, who would like to assume leadership roles, who would like to foster the growth and development of other teachers. Those she resents—the teachers who are unwilling to consider new roles or to work in partnership with other teachers without additional pay—represent long-standing NEA attitudes that emerged from lengthy struggles to improve salaries. Many teachers believe that IST positions add to the class load of other teachers, and that the utilization of the IST positions almost guarantees a time commitment, whether it means giving up a planning period or attending meetings after school for which the teachers are not paid.

The issue is a tough one. Teachers who wish to undertake new leadership positions end up spending more time than they are contracted for. Learning new techniques requires a time commitment. The dilemma in this school was whether teachers should undertake new projects without additional compensation. Many believed that this weakened the bargaining stance of the whole group. Others believed it was their obligation. The argument affected both the ISTs in their positions and the rest of the teaching faculty in the school. If teacher leadership is to move forward, these two attitudes toward professional responsibility and contractual rights must be reconciled.

Troubleshooting the Demonstration Center Model

The original IST position was created by central office administrators to support teachers better in expanding their instructional
repertoire. The fact that Mary and Barbara designed a program they
believed would respond to the problems that existed in the previous
program from their perspectives as ISTs and then managed to
convince the administration to allow them to put the program in
place suggests that the teachers were able to influence decision
making in the school system more effectively than in either of the
other two districts in which I observed. In this case, the administration did not feel the necessity to control these positions, nor was it
opposed to allowing teachers to design and implement programs
based on their own expertise. This is a good example of the kind of
shared decision making recommended in current reports.

The fact that full-time teachers were not part of the re-creation
of these positions is an issue that remains to be considered. It is
symptomatic of the low regard in which "regular" teachers are held
by almost everyone else that in neither case did administrators or
the teacher leaders themselves think to consult with the larger body
of teachers.

Given that Mary and Barbara had redesigned their role based on
their own reflective critique, it would have seemed quite logical for
them to compare the new role to the old one at the end of the first
year as a means by which to continue their reflective analysis of the
role's effectiveness. However, Mary and Barbara appeared to be too
swamped to think about it. They were preparing to attend an
evaluative retreat with two university professors, Janice, and a central office person. Again, no one from their building was asked to
participate. The focus of that retreat was to be on integrated instruction—whether it had worked or not, what they needed to change.
Justifiably, they were interested to know whether the methods they
were using with students were effective. However, no plans were
mentioned that would deal with whether the center was serving its
purpose as a demonstration site. The fact that they had been so
reflective before kept me hoping that they would continue to be so
with the new role they had created.

The other strikingly ironic factor was that although Mary and
Barbara redesigned their teacher leadership role, both had forgotten

to think through whom and how they would lead. Thus, teachers created leadership roles to bring about instructional improvement for other teachers without giving more than casual thought to how their colleagues would access the center. Because they were teachers themselves, one might have expected them to have heightened sensitivity to the full teaching schedules, to the inadequate time for preparation, to the lack of support their colleagues had to observe other teachers. It is possible that Mary and Barbara had forgotten the exigencies of the teaching day, since they had not been in the classroom for 4 years prior to their return to the demonstration center.

Clearly, the demonstration site was only a year old and was not yet functioning the way they hoped it would. This was compounded by the fact that the administration had asked them to keep quiet about what they were doing, so the rest of the teaching staff could not critique the role with very much authority. These beginners' dilemmas notwithstanding, other problems with this particular model were still quite apparent. A number of questions begged for consideration: How was the demonstration site to provide meaningful leadership for teachers busy with their own projects and, at this point, not committed to integrative instruction? How might teachers working alone in their classrooms translate Mary and Barbara's circumstances into their own rooms? Is it legitimate for the demonstration center to have more resources than other classrooms? Whereas the first model of teacher leadership was designed to be available to all teachers, this second model was less accessible to others. How might Mary, Barbara, and the administrators provide time for other teachers to utilize the demonstration center? Clearly, at the time of this study, Mary and Barbara were involved in an enormously challenging effort and were working the bugs out of their own experimental teaching. Still, if the model were to provoke change in other adults, and if others were to support funding for the program, these questions would have to be answered.

CHAPTER 6

Looking Across the Cases

Teacher leaders have to be advocates for teaching and teachers.
—Mary Jones

Each of these teacher leadership roles is unique. Each has its own set of assumptions, its own rationale, its own design for improving instruction. Acknowledging the differences, once I looked across the three I noted a number of constraints, supports, and other important issues common to at least two of them. I believe the identification of these similarities has the potential to inform the current movement to create more powerful teacher leadership positions in the future and to make significant gains in quality education. Again, it is important to remember that three cases represent exploratory work. Because of the vast differences among the cases, oftentimes similarities crossed only two of them. As a result, any insights that seem to emerge here need to be examined against the experiences of many teachers in a variety of contexts.

THE CONSTRAINTS AND SUPPORTS OF TEACHER LEADERSHIP

The teacher leaders and their colleagues identified both constraints and supports that influenced their work to improve education. Constraining factors hampered their ability to improve instruction and to meet the goals of the leadership positions. Supporting factors enabled them to engage in collaborative relationships and to recognize the gains they did make. Ironically, in almost all cases,

136

those conditions that provided support also were constraints. The provision of time and the lack of it is a case in point. Teacher leaders were given time to work with their colleagues—a tremendous support—but also agreed that the time allocated was inadequate. They needed more. Different players had different interpretations of the leadership roles and, as a result, looked for different kinds of assistance from the teacher leaders. Some interpretations were helpful, whereas others hindered the teacher leaders from doing the kind of work they believed should be done. Collaboration provides another example. The teacher leaders loved the opportunity to collaborate with others, and yet felt lonely as their roles separated them from their colleagues. In another instance, the teacher leaders described the enormous professional growth they experienced as a result of working with their colleagues. At the same time, their roles required them to know a good deal about change—a topic about which they knew little. Identification of constraining and supporting factors helps to clarify the strengths and weaknesses of these positions.

Time

Time is one of these paradoxes—at once a help and a hindrance. All three of these leaders taught only half time so that they might have the opportunity to work with other teachers. The additional time without students made their work with adults possible. All three mentioned how important it was for them to have regularly scheduled time that they could use in flexible ways. Both Mary and Gwen talked about their own dreams before they had "flex" time, when they were teaching a full day; every September they made a commitment to try something new, to collaborate with others, but their good intentions died away to silent whispers in the face of the demands of a full teaching schedule. All of them felt that they had been able to actually carry things out, to bring a few dreams to fruition because of the extra time.

At the same time, their most pervasive problem was time, and it limited each of the leaders in a variety of ways. Ted noted that time away from his students hampered his ability to give them the very best educational experience possible. All three found that they did not have enough time to fulfill their leadership responsibilities as well as they would have liked. Ted noted that they did not have

enough time to work with colleagues within the regular school day—
that it was not a norm, it was not something they planned for. He
would have liked fewer demands from the outreach networks, which
would have allowed him more time with students and with his
colleagues. Mary noted that the additional roles were added onto full-
time responsibilities without adequate consideration of the time it
takes to do these things well or to teach well. She believed that she
and Barbara had done a poor job of estimating the time it would take
them to prepare their classes and then run the center. Gwen felt
pressed by the extra responsibilities that were added to her IST
position. Both Mary and Gwen would have liked more time for their
own training. All of them would have liked more time to plan, to be
thoughtful.

Multiple Interpretations of Teacher Leadership

Everyone in the educational community had a different interpretation of the teacher leader's role, its purpose, and how the time
allocated should be spent. Three groups surfaced as critical—administrators, colleagues, and the local professional association. In some
cases, the various interpretations each of these groups developed
were helpful, but in others they were not.

Administrative interpretation of the positions was very important
to all three. Ted phrased it this way: it was important for the administrators to stay out of his way, not to interfere with his work, but at the
same time, he felt that it was important for them to value the work—
to see it as meaningful. Mary and Gwen were cognizant that their
positions would not exist unless the administrators believed them
important. Mary frequently referred to the administrators in her district with great respect. She felt that she learned a great deal from
them and that their input strengthened her ability to work with others.

Gwen believed that her role was constrained by the administrators' interpretation of it. Gwen's role had been interpreted by Vivian
as an administrative assistant position, which absorbed an enormous
amount of Gwen's time. Mary faced a different dilemma. The administrators in her building seemed to believe that the demonstration
center was an experimental project, not designed to influence the
other teachers in the building: hence their requests that Mary and
Barbara keep their work rather quiet.

In addition, both Gwen and Mary noted that teachers' interpretations of their positions proved constraining or enabling. If teachers perceived that the teacher leader's role was to function as an expert who had been selected to fix their teaching problems, if they believed that the teacher leader functioned as an arm of the administrative evaluation, then they were less open to having the teacher leaders in their rooms. Conversely, if teachers believed that the role was for their benefit, they were much more willing to collaborate. From another perspective, if teachers believed that these roles were designed to provide them with catch-up time, and asked the teacher leaders to cover their classes while they marked papers or went to an appointment, this, too, was constraining.

A third interpretation of the role important to the teacher leaders' ability to feel successful was that of the National Education Association (NEA). All of the teacher leaders with whom I work were in NEA states and belonged to their state affiliates and their local chapters. Ted had been given a teacher-of-the-year award by the state affiliate and believed that they were most supportive of the work he was doing. Gwen and Mary, in their administratively created, more formal roles, felt somewhat differently.

Gwen's association was opposed to the IST positions on the grounds that pulling a teacher out of the classroom increases the class size of every other teacher in the building and reduces everyone's possible effectiveness. Every year the association attempted to negotiate the positions out of the contract and every year the administrators firmly protected them, so from the beginning the positions were perceived by the association as administrative padding. The association opposed the positions on the class-size issue and also because it did not believe they provided legitimate support for teachers. Nor had the association been involved in either the creation or the design of these positions. As Gwen mentioned in the portrait, the association had sent out a questionnaire asking whether teachers would like to continue the IST positions or whether they would prefer another planning period. Though there was no doubt that the teachers wanted the planning time, the administrators continued to hold firm and maintained the leadership positions at the bargaining table.

Mary's association took a quieter stance, partially because the labor/management relations were far better in her district. The district executive director for the association and the deputy superintendent had worked for 2 years to negotiate contract language that supported participatory decision making for teachers. Their efforts, at this point in time, appear to be among the most productive and innovative in the country. As a result of the good relations, the association was neither wildly supportive nor outwardly resistant to the IST positions, even though it, like the association in Gwen's district, had no part in the creation or design of the positions. Still, Mary and the other ISTs did not believe that the association did anything to actively support their position. Nor did they believe they had anyone they could turn to to represent their interests should they run into any kind of difficulty with the administration.

At this point, the NEA has no policy on teacher leadership or on the roles that exist. The NEA's primary focus has been to negotiate bread-and-butter issues—salaries, compensation, length of work day, and so forth; their stance regarding teacher leadership appears to be that role differentiation undermines the power of collective bargaining (Wasley, 1988). Several cases demonstrate the NEA's opposition to role differentiation. The Tennessee Career Ladder program, which had the support of the state legislature and the state administration association, among others, was demolished by the state affiliate with the full support of the NEA. According to one source, the NEA spent more money on dismantling this program than on any other effort (Finn, 1985). In formal policy, and in recent studies, the NEA continues to distinguish between management functions and teacher functions (Bacharach, 1987). At the moment, it appears that when the local NEA interpretation suggests leadership positions do not disturb collective bargaining, the positions are supported. Otherwise, they are not supported and may be actively opposed.

On the other hand, the NEA has been exploring different leadership possibilities for teachers through their Mastery in Learning project and through the identification of new learning laboratories. Their projects are structured so that teachers in a building determine their particular areas of interest related to teaching and then engage in collaborative investigation. Frequently a teacher is released in order to coordinate the activities of the larger group. In addition, the NEA has sponsored a number of symposia and forums on the issue of teacher leadership (Livingston, 1991).

Interpretations of the roles Ted, Gwen, and Mary held were influenced by the quality of communication between all parties involved. All of the leaders mentioned that communication between them and other teachers about what it was that they were trying to do was extremely limited and haphazard. In the formal roles, information seemed to flow hierarchically from top to bottom, with little consideration given to communication among the teachers and the teacher leaders or to administrators from teacher leaders. Communication with the association in Mary's and Gwen's cases took place either at the bargaining table or between administrators, but not between the leaders and their association, or fellow members. Such communication may have done a great deal to create the resistance to their roles. Without question, communication seems to be central to the success of these roles—especially because much of it is privileged information. Furthermore, although administrative interpretations of the roles appeared to be more binding, the covert interpretation of the roles done by "regular" teachers was equally powerful.

Collegiality and Loneliness

All three of the leaders talked about how much they enjoyed the opportunity to work with other adults after years of working primarily with children. All of them spoke about how much they learned from others. Ted believed that he got as much from others as they did from him and that the collaborative time really helped to hone his ideas. Mary and Gwen felt that the time spent with other adults allowed them to talk about their work in reflective ways for the first time. All of them felt less isolated, less alone.

Conversely, Mary, Gwen, and Ted mentioned that as a result of their positions, they at times felt more lonely. In a traditionally isolating profession, once they assumed leadership positions, all these teachers found themselves even more isolated than they had previously. Mary's isolation was somewhat relieved by the strong collaborative relationship she had developed with Barbara, but she felt a great separation from much of the rest of the staff. Ted saw himself as part of a larger team, the Talking Mountain staff, but consistently felt the burden of being the chief worrier and the idea champion for all of them. Gwen held the only formal teacher leadership role in her building and felt very isolated at times. All of them talked about the fact that they existed in a kind of no-man's land— not plain faculty, not pure administrator; it was uncharted ground, unfamiliar and lonely.

Professional Growth and a Lack of Training

Mary, Ted, and Gwen all talked about their own professional growth that occurred as a result of these positions. Each gained a greater understanding of the complexity of the educational enterprise. Each gained insights into the variety of ways in which teachers work with students. Each had the opportunity to work with a variety of outside experts, which helped them to clarify their own ideas. The growth they experienced was directly related to the opportunities they had to work in these different circumstances, and all of them acknowledged that these opportunities fueled their commitment to public education and made them feel more professional.

At the same time, their preparation to work with their colleagues seemed incomplete. All had excellent training in their specialty areas. Ted had studied Dewey during his master's program, and because it fit with his personal teaching experience, he had studied Dewey's work thoroughly and now used it as the philosophical undergirding of his methodology. Gwen had had innumerable courses in Madeline Hunter's ITIP and had taught courses in it herself, so was thoroughly versed. Mary had had training in cooperative learning, "Math Their Way," whole-language instruction, and interdisciplinary learning, among others. She felt privileged to have had such excellent training.

On the other hand, none of them had had any exposure to the literature on educational change, which deals primarily with the implementation of innovation, to the work on leadership that suggests different ways to approach change, or to the material on conflict resolution that has emerged out of labor-management negotiations. In addition, they lacked information on how to work in groups, how to diagnose the needs of their colleagues and the school, and how to read the culture of the school. As a result, they had little understanding of how other adults felt about their suggestions, nor did they have the awareness of other ways in which they might have approached their colleagues.

Doing Both: Teaching and Leading

A major consideration in teacher leadership discussions is whether teachers should retain some classroom responsibility or whether they should be on full-time release. Gwen, Mary, and Ted believed that their teaching considerably enhanced their credibility with other teachers. In addition, all of them wanted to teach. Teaching for both Mary and Ted was the best part of their job. Because all three positions were designed to influence other teachers to change their teaching behavior in some way, all agreed that their firsthand experience with students made teachers far more likely to accept what they had to say. Mary said:

> I think it has to do with credibility as much as anything. It seems that once a teacher leaves the classroom to take on other leadership responsibilities, even though they're related to classroom teaching, other classroom teachers feel that that person is different from them in some way . . . and so doesn't really have a true understanding of what reality is in the classroom.

Ted noted that his personal experience bridged the gap between theory and practice, and that it is "unbelievably illogical" to have people teaching teachers who have no understanding of the complexity of schools. He noted, too, that for teachers, a love of teaching is a very important thing and helps to encourage change. In both Mary's and Gwen's districts, teacher leadership roles were stepping stones into administration and, therefore, the release time was very important. At the same time, the teaching experience was very important to establish trust and rapport with teachers.

Mary provided another view on the value of personal classroom work. In her experience, going into other people's rooms was an ineffective means of modeling a given instructional technique because teachers found it difficult to switch roles from teacher to learner in their own rooms. By allowing them the opportunity to visit another room, Mary believed that switch was easier. In addition, being able to work with a class on an ongoing basis allowed teacher leaders to establish their own rules and routines and to maintain a relationship with students so they could better assess the effects of the innovations they were trying.

At the same time, trying to both teach and lead created its own tensions. Both Ted and Mary were emphatic that the students in their classes always came first, so if anything suffered, it was their leadership responsibilities. In this way, teaching detracted from leading. Gwen mentioned several times that she felt a tremendous pull between the needs of the students and the demands of her extra responsibilities. Both Ted and Gwen mentioned that their students became resentful if they were gone from their classroom responsibilities too often. Ted and Mary noted that their extra responsibilities caused them to work longer hours. They had to prepare lessons as well as answer the requirements of their additional responsibilities.

On the other hand, their leadership responsibilities added to their teaching in several important ways. All three of the teacher leaders taught courses for other teachers to explain what it was that they did. They found this enormously beneficial. Gwen explained that before and during any class she teaches, she is submerged in a complex analysis. She studies how it is that she uses ITIP; she recognizes techniques she uses in different ways. As she attempts to teach what she knows to others, she again analyzes it for clarity. In all, her own understanding grows enormously, which then improves her ability to teach. Ted felt that he often picked up as many ideas from the teachers in his classes as he gave them. And, he reinforced Gwen's explanation:

> The act of trying to take them through some thinking about what it is we're doing together makes me think, too. Of course, I do that all the time anyhow, but doing it in a little more conscious way, structured way. Okay today we set aside 4 hours and all we do is think. This is it. You can't put it off. . . . When I teach a course and I really have time to prepare for it—do some background research and really set it up right, it's great.

Mary described the collective effects of her leadership role on her classroom teaching: "One of the neatest things about this year is I'm a better teacher than I have ever been. I can feel that in myself." The position provided her with a variety of opportunities that strengthened her teaching. First, she had excellent training through the district. Second, she had the opportunity to work collaboratively with the other ISTs to solve how best to help other teachers. Third, she had the opportunity to meet and speak with central office administrators. In addition, she worked with university professors. These collaborative experiences caused her to believe that she was a better teacher than ever.

MAJOR ISSUES

In addition to the constraints and supports that affected teacher leadership, a number of very important issues surfaced. All of these issues affected the teacher leaders' ability to lead others toward improved practice. Most of the teacher leaders and their colleagues had not given much thought to teacher leadership, how it might be defined, or what it might look like in practice, and so found the consideration of the roles in their midst a challenge. Two of the teacher leaders focused their work on instructional concerns, whereas the third spent a good deal of her time doing administrative kinds of work. Although both kinds of work are important to schools, faculties might benefit from shared understanding about the kinds of work the teacher leadership role encompasses. Perhaps the most important issue deals with who creates, selects, and evaluates teacher leaders. In no cases were the teachers who were to benefit from the roles involved in these processes. Another issue, the context in which each of these people worked, also had a significant impact on the teacher leader's ability to influence the practice of others—one role could not easily be transported to another place without giving careful thought to the impact of the place and its culture. Finally, all three of the teacher leaders engaged in collaborative working relationships. Scrutiny revealed that these took three distinct forms— mentoring, division of labor, and partnering. Each form of collaboration required different kinds of interactions between the teachers and suggested various assumptions about the nature of teaching, leading, and learning. Consideration of these major issues is necessary to a deeper understanding of teacher leadership and its possibilities.

Defining Teacher Leadership

In each of the schools that I visited, I asked teachers, teacher leaders, and administrators alike to define teacher leadership for me.

All of the teachers reacted similarly: "What do you mean? Department heads? Team leaders? Faculty room informal leaders?" Administrators often mentioned shared leadership or empowerment but were not more specific than that, other than to note that teachers had been playing leadership roles in their districts ever since they could remember. When I pushed for greater specificity, everyone was vague. They described teacher leaders as people who had the ability to share information and to influence others in matters related to curriculum and instruction. Leaders had the ability to go beyond the classroom to be current in research, and to be teaching advocates. Mary said that she believed teacher leadership meant having the ability to move forward toward a better system rather than simply supporting the existing system. Ted noted that teacher leaders were people who could work with kids so that kids pushed themselves beyond normal expectations.

When I asked them what kinds of roles they would create, none of the teachers I visited with suggested the positions that existed in their schools except the administrators. The teacher leaders called for a wider variety of roles that would allow more teachers the opportunity to participate. The colleagues called for roles that focused on instructional support—both paraprofessional support and the support of a teacher who could help gather important and energizing materials to challenge students. A teacher gave examples:

> I am doing a unit right now on Central America. Our text is really limited. If I had the time, I'd scour the university library, find music, posters, films, a couple of gorgeous picture books. I'd look for stuff on the rain forest—maybe have the kids write for information about the conditions in the jungle. The problem is after teaching all day long, and attending a meeting or two, I barely have time to get home, fix dinner for my family, and grab a couple of hours of planning time around my dining room table. I would love to be able to work with someone else who would help me gather better resources.

In addition, teachers wanted to be more involved in the decisions that affected their work in dealing with students.

The most striking and the most wrenching comment came from virtually all the people with whom I visited: They had never been

asked to define teacher leadership before, nor had they had a conversation about it in their professional lives. They had never in any
context been asked to consider how they might improve their profession, or what they might do to build stronger leadership among their
teaching fellowship. Granted that there are many ways to improve
schools, and that the discussions of teacher leadership is not the only
way, but the fact that teachers have not thought about these issues
provides a powerful example of both the isolation in which they
work and their lack of participation in the larger discussion about
their role in improving schools.

Clearly the whole issue of defining teacher leadership is problematic in that it has not been perceived as important in any aspect
of teacher preparation or continuing education. Nor has it been
significant enough to gain any full faculty discussion in schools.
Generating any kind of definition is further complicated by union
positions and collective bargaining. Since the establishment of collective bargaining, teaching has been an egalitarian profession;
every teacher in the system has equal rights and equal stature,
distinguished only by years of service and by hours of graduate credit
taken. Teachers are paid according to the number of years of service
and the number of degrees held rather than on the basis of role
differentiation. The only differentiated role that has been in place
for any stretch of time is that of department head, and few people
perceive those to be meaningful leadership positions. To a certain
degree, then, the discussion of teacher leadership assaults the egalitarian norms that have long been in place in teaching. Although my
original intention was to find out how teachers and teacher leaders
themselves would define teacher leadership, the reality seems to be
that they do not yet have a definition because it has never been
possible and/or meaningful to spend the time talking about it.
When they do define it, because it is an unfamiliar topic, they tend
to characterize teacher leadership in terms of their own work, which
does not necessarily provide a broad enough view for the overall
improvement of education.

Administrative Work or Instructional Work

Ted, Mary, and Gwen each spend a certain percentage of time
working on instructional issues. Other time is spent on administra-

tive work. Ted devoted about a quarter of his time to administrative work for his own corporation, raising money, documenting progress, and solving personnel problems. He spent virtually no time working on administrative issues related to his school. Because he created his own position, he was able to determine where he would put his energies and, as a result, most of his time was taken up by issues related to curriculum and instruction.

Gwen's situation was quite different. She held a position created and evaluated by her administrators. She was constantly asked to fulfill a variety of administrative tasks, as mentioned earlier. During the 2 weeks I was with Gwen, she had approximately 20 hours scheduled to work with teachers. In the eight interactions she had with other teachers during that 2-week period, she spent less than 3 hours total working with them. She and I estimated that there might be an additional 2 or 3 hours spent writing observations, but she used the rest of her time meeting with the representatives from social service agencies, acting as principal, working to organize assemblies and teas, and disciplining students. Gwen did not feel that she had the authority to change the amount of time she spent on administrative work, although she believed that other teachers saw it and resented it. They were told that the position was to support their needs when clearly it was not. Gwen felt that she was between a rock and a hard place.

Mary's position was created to respond to teachers. When they appeared to mistrust the role, she re-created the position so that she worked with students half the time. Mary, like Ted, spent the majority of her time working on issues related to curriculum and instruction and a minimum amount fulfilling administrative tasks.

In these three instances, the two teacher leaders who had some say in the design of their positions managed to work on curriculum and instruction, whereas the administratively designed role demanded more time to support administrative work. The important issue is not the legitimacy of administrative support, or that administrators legitimately have more to do than they can possibly accomplish, but the consistency or the integrity with which these positions are created and then implemented.

A solution might be to create two types of leadership positions: one that supports instructional work and another which supports administrative work. Those who choose to focus on instruction might be teachers who have no intentions of leaving the classroom. Those who choose administrative work may be in the process of considering a move to administration. This seems to me to be a more appropriate and direct approach.

The Creation, Selection, and Evaluation of Teacher Leadership Positions

Mary, Gwen, and Ted were all affected by the processes used to design their roles, to select them, and to evaluate them. These three components are critical and dramatically influence teacher leaders' ability to work with others and to influence the nature of the work. Consideration of the three reveals how complex and intertwined each of these processes is.

The original creation of the roles influenced who had power, authority, and autonomy to determine how the role might function and how time would be spent. Ted created his own position, which evolved out of his success in working with students. Gwen's position was created by the superintendent and then was interpreted in each building by the principal. Mary's position was created by district office personnel, although she was allowed to redesign it to support better learning. Because they created or redesigned their own positions, both Ted and Mary had more authority and autonomy than Gwen, whose position was particularly vulnerable to administrative delegation. Because Ted's position had nothing to do with the regular running of the school, he had far greater autonomy and far less dependence on administrators than either Mary or Gwen. Ted often said that if they gave him any trouble at all, he could easily pull the team out of the district and move to another school nearby, as he had been invited to move numbers of times. Gwen, on the other hand, had no control over her position and so found it necessary to continue to depend on her principal. Conversely, Mary believed that her administrators supported her position, but because of the movement to building-based decision making, she felt that the teachers might well jeopardize her position. Because the authority had been taken away from the central office administrators who created the positions, she felt less than secure.

The processes used to select teacher leaders are important because they influence the response to the position from the viewpoints of both the administration and the teaching faculty. If faculty perceive the teacher leader to be either anointed or appointed by the administration, the teacher leader almost immediately loses credibility. In the two cases where teacher leaders were selected by administrators, the response of colleagues was more troublesome when the principal did the choosing than it was when a team of administrators did so in a district-wide search process. However, both administratively selected positions were more troublesome than the position in which selection was not done by administrators.

Evaluation of the teacher leadership positions was equally important in determining whether the role was really influencing change. Ted was not evaluated for his leadership role unless he arranged for it, which he did frequently. He had evaluations done by the teachers who took his classes. He hired an outside evaluator to conduct interviews with teachers who had taken his courses to see whether the courses and the networks had any kind of long-term effect. That study was ongoing so that he could ascertain the effects of the courses and the networks over time. Within his school district, his teaching was evaluated by the principal, like that of every other teacher.

Mary and Gwen had different kinds of evaluations, but similar to Ted's teaching evaluation. Their leadership responsibilities were assessed by their superiors—Mary's by the director of curriculum, Gwen's by her principal. In both cases the evaluations were conducted much like teaching evaluations in that there was a preconference where the evaluator and the "evaluatee" established what it was that the teacher leader would work on for the year. The postconference was designed to ascertain whether the goals set in the preconference had been met. In neither case was the evaluation designed to check on the effectiveness as it affected the other teachers or students. The fact that evaluations were conducted in this manner supported the assumption that the supervisors of the roles believed that they were better equipped than the teacher leaders' colleagues to tell whether the model was working or not.

In the design, selection, and evaluation of these positions, the most disturbing silence is in the voice of the teachers these roles are intended to support. No teachers were involved in any of these processes in Ted's, Mary's, or Gwen's schools. The fact that teachers were uninvolved had a direct and negative impact on the effects of the positions.

The Importance of Context

Each of these teacher leadership positions is firmly rooted in a particular context that takes into account the school and its participants, the community, the state and region. That context is critically important to the success or failure of the role. If, for instance, one looked at Gwen's role without adequate understanding of the context, one might assume that her colleagues were not satisfied with the position because she lacked skill. Given this attitude, Gwen might be sent back to the classroom to be replaced by another anointed teacher. It is unlikely that any teacher would be successful in this particular context. Without a thorough understanding of the context, one might also assume, as did many of the administrators in this district, that teachers are uninterested in leadership opportunities and in extending themselves professionally. This, too, could not be further from the truth.

In the same vein, if one looked only at Ted's role through the university classes he teaches, one would miss the importance of his own classroom experience and the fact that he had been allowed to change his working circumstances within a traditional setting so that he could engage in teacher outreach centers. Ted himself indicated that if the administration in his school had prevented him from establishing and running Talking Mountain, he might well have left public education long ago.

Similarly, if one visited Mary's classroom—because it is such a stimulating and exciting place—the first inclination might be to race back and create a similar kind of demonstration site. Such a replication might well re-create the kinds of tensions between the faculty and the teacher leaders that exist in Mary's building.

Each site had its own distinct culture. It is unlikely that Gwen's model of teacher leadership could be exported to Mary's school. Nor is it likely that Ted's model could be transplanted to Gwen's school until some work had been done on the existing constraints on teacher leadership in her building. In each case, the conception of teacher leadership and the development and the implementation of each of the roles was contextually bound.

Kinds of Collaboration

The teacher leaders were involved in different kinds of collaborative work. Each type had different requirements and assumptions and communicated different messages about teachers and teaching. Whereas Ted was engaged in mentoring and Gwen in a division-of-labor collaboration, Mary was involved in partnering. Each of these kinds of collegiality was distinctly suited to particular kinds of working circumstances, and each of the teacher leaders in the study worked with more than one kind of collaborative relationship in his or her school.

Mary, Gwen, and Ted all had mentoring responsibilities. As mentors, the shared assumption was that they had some expertise to share with colleagues who lacked it. Sometimes this worked well; other times it created tension and professional jealousy, and shut down the potential for the working relationship. For instance, when Gwen observed a teacher who was interested in fostering a democratic classroom, her suggestions about creating the appropriate anticipatory set—regardless of how useful this might be—seemed irrelevant and condescending to her colleague. When Mary invited the colleague who was interested in integrated learning into her classroom to see what she and Barbara were doing, there appeared to the colleague little room for her to share what she had been working on for the last several years. She felt diminished rather than supported by the experience. When the special education teacher in Ted's school decided to try his methodology with her students, she felt very supported in her experimentation because she could run down to Ted's room to share what she'd been doing and could ask him for help quickly and easily.

Mentoring also takes a toll on the mentor. Ted mentioned frequently that although he felt it worked well, mentoring left him exhausted and emotionally depleted. Mary shared that she sometimes found it very difficult to distill how her years of experience led her to particular practices. Gwen felt that the trick was to validate the teacher's personal experience while encouraging him or her to try new techniques. Teachers often became defensive and felt threatened by the mentoring relationship. Gwen also noted that it was difficult to build enough trust to allow for a good exchange to take place.

In Gwen's library responsibilities, she and Janice divided up the labor. Both of them felt that the opportunity to share the responsibility for the library strengthened the programs offered, because neither of them had time to undertake it all. As a result, they worked together to divide their responsibilities and then worked alone fulfilling their tasks. Dividing the labor assumes that both people are professional, that there is too much work for one person, and that each will complete the assigned tasks with greater efficiency and effectiveness. This gave them the feeling of collaborating, and gave each a partner with whom to exchange ideas, but did not require that they actually agree on the way individual tasks were carried out, or even communicate with each other about how they were doing things. Not only does it reduce the isolation, but it is also easier than other forms of collaboration because it requires limited shared decision making and limited examination of individual practices.

Both Mary's and Gwen's roles were designed so that they mentored other teachers, and Mary also engaged in equal partnering with her colleague, Barbara. The two of them shared responsibility for curriculum development, for lesson planning, and for evaluating the success of their experimentation. They both generated suggestions for curricular units and talked through how they might do each unit. When one person agreed that she would take responsibility for a particular piece—as Mary did in creating the writing segments of their integrated units—she brought those back to the other, explained them, and then the two of them worked on the plan until they both agreed that it was the kind of instructional tool they both could support. This partnering was more complex than dividing up the labor and required significantly more time to work together. It assumed that they were both professionals, but that by engaging in shared decision making and consensus about everything they were to teach, they would strengthen the curriculum and instructional tools generated. Each unit was the product of two people's thinking rather than one person's. They both felt richly rewarded by this partnering relationship and believed that it provided additional incentives for their work. It was this kind of collegiality that seemed the most rewarding. Both Barbara and Mary believed that it provided the kinds of incentives to keep them interested in teaching and growing as professionals, while helping them to be more effective with kids. It was the kind Ted longed for most but found infrequently. (For a more thorough discussion of the differences inherent in the three kinds of collaborative relationships and their relationship to teacher leadership, see Wasley, 1991.)

As I looked back across these three cases, I was struck again at how enormously complex teacher leadership roles are as they play out in practice. They involve power, authority, and decision-making relationships as well as different kinds of collaborations; and they communicate beliefs and attitudes about the nature of teaching and learning. Those factors that enabled the teacher leaders to be successful with their colleagues also constrained them, at once enhancing and diminishing their potential effectiveness. Further, the examinations of the three cases reveal a number of important issues that prompt the necessity for some careful thinking about how teacher leadership positions might be strengthened to make schools more powerful and engaging places for both the adults and the students who spend time in them. In the last chapter, I review what I think these cases reveal to us: the problems, the paradoxes, and the possibilities of teacher leadership.

CHAPTER 7

Problems, Paradoxes, and Possibilities

As I thought about Ted, Mary, and Gwen in their individual contexts, a number of images were illuminated for me from my own days in a leadership role. As I listened to Gwen quietly admit that she was uncertain about how others felt about her role, to Mary's anger at her colleagues' unprofessional attitudes, and to Ted as he talked about how exhausting it is to try to both teach and lead, I seemed to be hearing myself discussing just such concerns with my own colleagues in our little office years ago. At the same time, when each of the three of them described the enormous growth they'd experienced as a result of the opportunity to work in different ways, I recognized what had motivated me as well. As I mulled what I learned from the three positions, my first inclination was to agree with Devaney's (1987) claim that the positions that exist are too problematic and should be dismissed or dismantled in order to start from scratch. My second inclination was to recognize that although these positions are in fact full of problems and riddled with paradoxes, they are also rich in possibilities. Any kind of wholesale dismissal would be simplistic and might well result in the re-creation of similar positions with similar problems. Seymour Sarason (1972) says, "Unless the compass that guides us has history built into it, we will go in circles, feel lost, and conclude that the more things change, the more they stay the same. . . . One can only sigh and say, 'Here we go again' when we see efforts to shape futures based on rejection or ignorance of the past" (p. 22). Ted, Gwen, and Mary taught me a good deal about the kinds of considerations that should be taken into account when building new teacher leadership positions or redesigning old ones. In the remainder of this chapter, I examine first the major problems and paradoxes of teacher leadership and then suggest how I might go about experimenting with the possibilities for future positions.

THE PROBLEMS

Examination of these three cases revealed a number of problems inherent in these particular positions. Whether they plague all current teacher leadership positions remains to be seen as more cases are investigated. However, an understanding of the problems that arose for Tom, Gwen, and Mary has been important to my thinking about how to proceed with new teacher leadership positions. Among the difficulties that need resolving are determining whether the intentions for the positions match the realities, whether there are real incentives, whether teachers are really participating in the discussion, and what kinds of attitudes and assumptions the roles created communicate about teaching and learning. Furthermore, the relationship between administrators and teacher leaders needs attention.

Matching Intentions with Realities

Once a leadership position is created, it is seldom reevaluated to determine whether the actual practice matches the original intentions. In all three cases, those who conceived of the teacher leader positions believed that they provided a way to improve the quality of educational experiences students received by giving teachers a greater role in the educational enterprise. However, with the exception of Ted, they neglected to assess whether the role accomplished its purposes.

Ted's model of teacher leadership was designed to provide teachers with the opportunity to collaborate with others interested in pedagogical change. Teachers who chose to join the teacher outreach networks were provided with opportunities to write, to teach other adults, and to share their own experiences. Thus, they were less isolated and also enabled to interpret the methodology with their own students in their own context. Students produced something—magazines, videotapes, environmental brochures—and these products helped teachers to evaluate the quality of their students' educational experiences. The teachers I talked with believed that their students were more motivated and were doing more sophisticated work than they had done previously. Outside evaluations conducted by contracted researchers indicated that students reported more powerful learning experiences and the development of skill at the same time. These evaluations also suggested that about 25% of the teachers who took the courses ended up adapting the pedagogy, whereas many others took the class but remained unaffected. For those teachers who continue to explore the pedagogy, it appears that the original intentions for Ted's role are achieved.

Gwen's teacher leadership role was also designed to produce improved educational experiences for students. Her model suggested that if all teachers used a series of generic teaching strategies, students would benefit. The teachers with whom I spoke either did not believe that there were any positive results for students or thought perhaps there were, but they weren't sure what—other than that teachers were clearer in the presentation of material. The model seemed designed to support teacher-centered teaching and other traditional approaches to instruction. There was no evidence of improved student performance, but no attempt to measure that had been made. Furthermore, the fact that Gwen was frequently diverted from working with teachers perhaps diluted the potential of the role to effect instructional change. An unspoken purpose of the position seemed to be administrative support, an aim that Vivian did not openly acknowledge although she did admit that Gwen was very helpful to her.

Mary's role, as redesigned by Mary, was formed to reduce traditional isolation for teachers as well as to improve student performance. The isolation she and Barbara had experienced in the classroom was all but gone. On the other hand, as it stood in the first year of the program, the teachers whom the role was intended to support were unaffected. They had to arrange their own visits, find someone to cover their classes, or give up planning periods in order to make visits. These arrangements made participation very difficult for them. Thus, in Mary's case, the isolation in which teachers worked was reduced only for those who held the leadership role. Initial findings from a study done on the effects of the demonstration classroom instruction suggested that students had a much more positive attitude toward learning while maintaining good standing on standardized tests. Student motivation seemed to have increased, which did provide an incentive for Mary and Barbara—willing students make better partners. No evaluation had been conducted among other teachers to determine whether their classroom practices were changed. Conversations I had with other teachers suggested that their instruction was not affected by Mary and Barbara's work, but then, again, it was still the first year of this new program. It seems fair to say that after the first year, half of the goals of this position were met—students were having more powerful experiences—whereas the other half—providing collaborative working conditions for teachers—were missed.

In order for teacher leadership roles to accomplish what they set out to do, teachers and administrators need to collaborate to build the purposes for the role so that these are clear to all involved. In order to assess whether the roles match the original intentions, evaluations must be conducted. If the purpose of the role is to improve student performance, student performance should be measured in some way. If the purpose is also to affect the pedagogical techniques of teachers, assessment should gauge whether teachers really use and believe in the techniques they've been encouraged to incorporate into their repertoire. The evaluation of these positions need not be formal nor necessitate hiring outside experts at great expense. A simple series of interviews, a survey, or a roundtable discussion at a faculty meeting where all affected can be included may do the trick. The most important aspect of such an assessment is that it should be conducted collaboratively so that everyone originally intended to be affected by the role is involved in working toward creating positions and opportunities that actually achieve their shared purposes.

Incentives for Teacher Leadership

Although they are seldom explicitly considered, incentives for both the teacher leaders and those being assisted help to determine the viability of the teacher leadership role and the breadth of participation by the teacher leader's colleagues. Incentives are problematic because they must exist for two groups, not just one. Ted's, Mary's, and Gwen's roles offer different incentives to both the teacher leaders and to their colleagues. The incentives for Ted to undertake a leadership position were powerful. First, his primary inducement came from his own students and what he believed were their far more powerful learning experiences. In addition, he was able to work with a large number of teachers, from whom he learned a great deal. He was also able to set the role up in any way he wished, so that it suited his particular aims, purposes, and schedule. He determined how much time he would teach and how much he would devote to the work of leading. The incentives for those who took his classes revolved around the opportunity to work with like-minded teachers and to see greater productivity in students. Opportunities were also available for those who wished to help teach the courses or write about their experiences. The incentives were less powerful for these teachers—they gave up their own time to participate and still worked in isolation within their own buildings. Few of them had explicit support from their administrators.

The incentives for Gwen were many. She had the opportunity to work with others, a flexible schedule, the ear of the principal, and the opportunity to watch others teach. The incentives for participation in the larger teaching faculty were considerably more limited. Half of the teachers I spoke with felt coerced. They had been told that they would participate regardless of their own beliefs or needs. Others said that the role gave them the opportunity to share what they were doing with another adult, but none of them indicated that the role had any effect on their own instruction. The principal also had incentives for retaining the position because it provided a vehicle for the delegation of other duties.

Mary's role provided great incentives for her and Barbara, but few for the larger faculty. Mary and Barbara shared, argued, and celebrated together when things went well. Their colleagues felt like peasants who enviously watch the activity at the manor house while working in the fields. In order to participate, they had to organize their schedules and their time—all on top of their own full teaching loads. The incentives for them were minimal, the disincentives considerable.

Teacher leadership positions should provide incentives to both the leaders and to those led. One without the other generates a role in which the teacher leader cannot succeed. If there are no incentives for the leaders, good people will not choose to take on the additional responsibilities. If there are no incentives for their colleagues, they will ignore the services offered. Consideration should also be given to the nature of the incentives. If the teachers with whom McLaughin and Yee (1988) worked are representative of other teachers, improved student performance and the opportunity to work collaboratively are the incentives teachers recognize as powerful and meaningful.

Teachers as Nonparticipants

Although these three cases illustrate that teacher leaders have the potential to be a valuable leadership resource, they also demonstrate that most teachers are unresponsive to top-down efforts to improve their instruction through administratively created teacher leadership positions. Futhermore, they have been nonparticipants in the discussion about teacher leadership. Teachers interviewed here had never been asked to discuss what constitutes a meaningful career. They had never been asked what they would do to improve the quality of their professional practice. They had not discussed what circumstances, conditions, and resources might enable them to see greater results in their teaching. They had not been asked by their professional association, by their administrators, by their college professors, or by their colleagues to examine what would attract more teachers to teaching, what might retain more teachers, what they believe would allow them to improve the quality of the educational experience their students receive. To a large degree, they were unaware of the current discussion about teacher leadership because that discussion was conducted in arenas outside their schools. They were unaware of the articles, the second-wave reform reports, and the limited research on teacher leadership because that information had not reached their practitioner's journals or the college courses that they were attending in order to update their credentials or to move up on the salary schedule. As a result, they did not know how they might define teacher leadership nor had they any practice in considering new possibilities.

The reasons for this nonparticipation are probably many. One might be that teaching takes place in bureaucracies where those at the bottom are seldom involved in central decision making and are frequently left out of the information loop. Perhaps collective bargaining has focused teachers on issues related to compensation rather than those related to the improvement of practice. It may be that teachers' knowledge of practice has long been discounted as too subjective, too nonscientific, so that teachers are not considered serious participants in the conversation about the improvement of practice. Therefore, the discussion takes place in journals and books that circulate to university faculty but not to the mailboxes or the coffee tables of school faculty lounges. Perhaps it is because legislatures have restricted teacher participation through mandated controls. And it may be that the public wants teachers to function in too many capacities—counselors, surrogate parents, intellectual guides, coaches—so there is not time left for participation in the discussion about teacher leadership.

For whatever reasons, these cases, coupled with the notable absence of teachers' voices in the literature, illustrate that teachers have not been included in the current discussion about teacher leadership despite the charge to involve them. In view of the extensive research indicating that meaningful change is unlikely when those affected by the change are uninvolved in the planning and implementation, this condition poses a serious problem to the improvement of the educational system.

Attitudes and Assumptions About Teaching and Learning

Each of the cases demonstrates that the role of the teacher leader communicates messages about the nature of teaching and learning to teachers, students, administrators, and the community. In Ted's case, his role—a regular classroom teacher teaching other teachers—assumes that any teacher who wants to can engage in experiential education. It also assumes that community involvement in the education of students is important, because all of the projects require that students work in the larger community in some way. Ted's role demonstrates that teaching is an interaction between teachers and students, something that must be left to their mutual investigation and interpretation. His role also conveys an attitude that teaching and learning require teachers and students to come together in the spirit of mutual inquiry and that they consider their relationship to the community in which they live.

Gwen's teacher leadership role—prescriptive teacher leadership—assumes that teaching and learning involve the act of presenting information from the learned to the unlearned. It suggests that teaching can be described in terms of several discrete skills that all teachers can use in order to better communicate information to their students. It also suggests that hierarchical decision making is more likely than participatory decision making to improve student learning. The attitude conveyed is that teaching is not particularly complex, or is at least definable.

Mary's role—teacher leadership through a demonstration center—assumes that good learning for students takes place in an atmosphere of collaboration and when subject matter is integrated rather than segregated. It suggests that for teachers to engage in learning, they must be freed from their own classroom responsibilities in order to participate as learners, and that teachers need to see changed practice in order to be motivated to change their own. It also assumes that individual teachers need to choose participation, and that they will take responsibility to organize their participation. The attitude conveyed is that teacher leaders are privileged—they have additional planning time, more resources, and more attention from administrators.

Current roles should be examined to determine what attitudes and assumptions they communicate about teaching and learning. Future teacher leadership roles should be constructed so that they convey positive, enabling attitudes and assumptions about teachers, about the nature of learning, and about what we hope for students.

The Role of Administrators

In all the cases, the role of administrators as they related to the teacher leadership positions was problematic. Clearly, the institution of teacher leadership positions was foreign to the administrators and left them a little uncertain about how best to support the roles. Given that these roles were created during a period when principals were touted as the instructional leaders in the building, the integration of the two positions had to be confusing. Nonetheless, examination of the roles indicates that they cannot reach their potential if they are not supported and understood by the administrators.

Ted's principal allowed Ted to fulfill his entrepreneurial role in the school without any other special consideration. Ted brought additional teachers into the system and paid for them out of Talking Mountain funds, which eased the financial constraints of their small rural system. However, Ted was evaluated just like everyone else and had to attend faculty meetings, monitor the halls, and fulfill lunch duties. Furthermore, the principal did not highlight what was going on in the Talking Mountain classrooms, nor did he encourage the rest of the faculty to become involved. He merely tolerated their existence and, it seemed to me, hoped that no more of these aberrations would crop up in his school.

Vivian clearly had a negative influence on the teacher leadership position in her school. She understood "teacher leadership" to be synonymous with delegation, which, of course, it is not. Vivian determined the kinds of instructional techniques that would be stressed and who would stress them with faculty. She calculated how many observations would be done and how feedback would be given, without any discussion with the teachers or the teacher leader. She believed that she knew best and that she was the best person to make these decisions. She then delegated a number of additional tasks that were more immediate and visible—like bus duty and the organization of awards assemblies—to Gwen, completely undermining her ability to work with teachers toward instructional improvement. Vivian did not ask for feedback, nor did she monitor the role closely so that she could make any accurate assessment of its effectiveness.

Gwen noted that Vivian was not open to suggestions and implied that she was punished for contradicting Vivian. Several other teachers mentioned Vivian's ability to make life uncomfortable if they did not comply with her requests. When I asked what they meant specifically by this, they indicated that they might be asked to take on the most unpleasant tasks or might be denied requests to attend conferences of interest. Since there was such agreement about Vivian in this regard, it was apparent to me that she would never get honest feedback from her staff, that her unwillingness to share decision making canceled her opportunity to create a position of any potential at all.

In Mary's case, the principal and the vice principal were at once supportive and constraining. They agreed to the significant design changes that Mary and Barbara requested. The administrators found them a school, worked out a schedule that allowed the two teachers to keep the students for a long block of time, and then provided them with computers and other materials they needed. They assisted them in assembling a heterogeneously mixed group of students and supported their requests to have visitors in from outside. What they didn't do was to assist Mary and Barbara in providing leadership opportunities for their colleagues. By telling the two teacher leaders to be quiet about their work, the administrators sabotaged the role significantly. In this case, they encouraged a kind of covert activity; they did not want the rest of the faculty to know enough about Mary and Barbara's project to challenge it or to make more demands on it. Although their actions appeared to be based on good intentions designed to protect the program, they actually undermined it.

The creation of teacher leadership roles means that teachers and principals must forge new working relationships and must be willing to share responsibility for instructional improvement in the building. Traditional modes of interaction—like delegation—are not real acts of shared leadership. In delegation, the person who holds the authority makes the decisions. In shared leadership, administrators, teacher leaders, and teachers share the decision making in order to determine how best to improve schooling for children and then how best to implement their mutual recommendations. Teachers and administrators must be able to have frank discussions about authority and accountability if teacher leadership roles are to have any potential whatsoever.

THE PARADOXES

In addition to the problems that surface in current teacher leadership positions, a number of challenging paradoxes become apparent. These are perhaps more difficult because they demonstrate the contradictory nature of our hope to improve schools while maintaining things the way they are. As with all paradoxes, recognition of them reinforces the unnerving complexity of attempts to change educational practice. I pose the bulk of the discussion in questions simply because the issues *are* complex and the answers are not yet apparent.

Shared Leadership in Hierarchical Systems

The whole discussion of teacher leadership is centered on the assumption that teachers need to be more involved in the decision making that takes place in their schools. And yet, schools are hierarchical systems. Most schools are organized as fundamental bureaucracies with hierarchical decision-making structures in place to facilitate efficiency and productivity. In Gwen's case, she was delegated the task of performing teacher leadership activities. She did not participate in the decision making about the creation or the design of the role. Using the term *leadership* in the context of her role might be a misnomer, because Gwen was really "led" by Vivian's contradictory directives. In Ted's case, he was able to negotiate his own working circumstances because he brought money and community support to the school. However, he still worked within the hierarchical decision-making chain within his building. Is it possible to create true leadership opportunities for teachers in the midst of hierarchical systems? If so, who will take the rap when things go wrong? Will teachers be offered the ability to take risks on behalf of their students and then be allowed to take responsibility for their actions? Can we create true leadership if both decision making and accountability are not present at the same time?

Mary's working circumstances suggest that she was able to orchestrate a shared decision-making structure. Rather than simply translating an administrative plan into action, she was able to reconceptualize and then redesign the actual role. What were the contingencies that made that possible? What does the organizational structure look like that allows for such flexibility? How is it that they have managed to convey to members of their community that teacher leaders have the authority to participate in questioning the existing system without encouraging anarchy and without appearing unfocused and chaotic? At the same time, is it possible to create teacher-designed positions that include the participation of all involved?

These cases demonstrate that without some measure of autonomy, some ability to make decisions on behalf of their colleagues—the teachers—teacher leaders cannot create effective positions, and without shared decision making, the roles are stripped of their potential power.

Overt/Covert Behavior Patterns

In the cases of Ted, Gwen, and Mary, examples of overt support but covert resistance to the work of teacher leaders surfaced. In Ted's case, the principal claimed to support his program but ignored the work the Talking Mountain staff was doing. Several teachers in the building who had taken Ted's class claimed that he was the best college course instructor they'd ever had but admitted among themselves that the methodology was not for them. In both Mary's and Gwen's cases, their colleagues appeared overtly to support their work, yet covertly found it meaningless, insulting, or problematic. In Gwen's case, the teachers indicated that they would be punished if they revealed their true feelings. In Mary's case, I believe that she and Barbara were really unaware of their colleagues' perceptions of their roles, and that they would have worked to change those perceptions had they known them. Overt sanctions joined to covert resistance do not allow for the kind of honest scrutiny and collaborative problem solving that might really strengthen these roles. At the same time, it created a false sense of success for the designers of the roles.

The questions these behaviors raise are tough: Is it possible to create teacher leadership positions that are supported by all those involved? Or, if that is too unrealistic, is it possible for people who disagree with a particular approach to do so publicly—and to choose participation or not based on their best professional judgment, without creating tensions and competitive divisions among the staff? Is it possible to create leadership positions that do not force teachers and administrators into overt sanctions of a position and covert rejection of it? Is it possible to develop procedures for designing and then evaluating teacher leadership positions that would foster open communication between those who are participating and those who aren't?

Learning from Colleagues

It is ironic in a profession directed toward fostering a love of learning throughout life that teachers themselves appear to have such a difficult time learning from their colleagues. Ted, Mary, and Gwen led me to conclude that the egalitarian ethos of teaching—the fact that all teachers hold equal position and rank, separated only by numbers of years of experience and college credits earned—makes it problematic for teachers to perceive their colleagues as experts. And yet, the whole concept of teacher leadership is based on the notion that teachers within their own school systems should be involved in the formulation of improvement efforts. Although Ted found it possible to influence teachers all over the country and the teachers in his building believed he was a good leader, he had little effect on the teaching methods of his colleagues in his own school. Although Mary was well respected throughout her district, she found her colleagues in her own building the most difficult to work with. And although Gwen taught college-level courses for teachers from her district, she frequently mentioned that she did not know how much effect she had on her fellow staff members.

Recent developments in public education may be responsible for this paradox. Although teaching has never been a differentiated profession, collective bargaining ensured all teachers uniform status. Given the history of equality within the profession, it is difficult for teachers to see each other any other way. Such circumstances, where teachers want the opportunity to influence their colleagues from a teacher's base but cannot gain authority or integrity unless they come from an unequal and hierarchical position, completely confound teacher leadership.

Another recent development may have contributed to the problem. Staff development programs designed to upgrade the skills of teachers generally encourage the notion that outside experts are best suited to encourage professional growth; the result is that insiders are not recognized as important or powerful (Lambert, 1988). In addition, familiarity with colleagues on a daily basis makes an "expert" stance more difficult. And yet, when asked what they would do to improve the quality of their professional practice, teachers in this study, as well as teachers across the country in a recent national survey, indicated that they want more time to learn from their colleagues (Bacharach, 1986).

The question may deal with the kind of roles created. Earlier we discussed how different kinds of collegiality suggest different assumptions about teaching and learning. It may be that when teachers say they want the opportunity to work together, they do not mean in mentoring relationships where one teacher is deemed an expert, the others novices. Perhaps their unclarified preference is for the chance to work in teams on issues of mutual interest, much like the teachers in the schools Little (1986) described or like Barbara and Mary in their school.

The conundrum remains: Will teachers recognize and accept leadership from someone who teaches next door? What are the circumstances of working together that teachers will support? What kind of culture needs to be in place to support teachers so they can recognize the expertise of their colleagues and grow from the opportunities to work with them?

These three paradoxes are critical to the possibilities for viable teacher leadership positions. Although the answers are not yet apparent or clear, faculties need to grapple with these questions so that they can begin to construct roles that are vibrant and powerful.

THE POSSIBILITIES

My study of these three teachers who lead, particularly within the context of the current rhetoric of reform, has provided me with a clearer view of the possible. I am both heartened by the potential for teacher leadership, and respectful of the complexity involved in any attempt to create stronger leadership roles for teachers. I also have a more realistic sense of what I'd choose to do, given the opportunity to build or redesign teacher leadership positions.

I am heartened because these cases demonstrate that teachers have enormous, nearly untapped creative resources to apply to the intransigent problems that plague their practice. Ted and the teachers who participate in the outreach networks have helped students to work hard in school, uncovering skills, fortitude, and drive that none of their other teachers knew the students had. By challenging passive instructional methods and by stretching the curriculum to encompass what interests students (rather than asking the students to succumb to a standardized distillation of state guidelines), he and his colleagues have provided a pedagogical philosophy toward which other teachers can work and at the same time interpret according to their discipline, their creativity, their context, and their collaborative investigations with students. By requiring that students produce some product of use to the local community, he has provided them with real connections to the world in which they live, and teachers with something tangible by which to assess the quality of student learning. By examining and reexamining his own educational philosophy and the means by which he acts upon that philosophy in the classroom, he has provided a model of reflective practice that has influenced teachers across the country. Ted's work makes real the vision of more challenging classrooms that public education teachers can create.

Mary's work demonstrates the kind of courage that many teachers need to challenge the existing system that does not support good learning for students. Mary and her partner rejected a role that was considered prestigious and was administratively sanctioned because they didn't think it worked. They returned to the classroom to see if they could influence others more powerfully by practicing what they had been preaching. They rejected standardized texts, an over-simplified and disconnected curriculum, bells that indicate that learning happens in 40 minutes, and duty-free recess times. They did this in favor of working longer hours to produce their own curriculum, and so that they might organize their classroom instructional time in a way better suited to student learning. They demonstrated a willingness to experiment and to do so in front of others. They pushed themselves to collaborate in a partnership built on consensus, requiring each of them to hold her beliefs and practices up to the scrutiny of the other. They demonstrated the kind of pioneering spirit so badly needed in schools if the world of real knowledge and the world of the classroom are to be connected.

Gwen offers another glimpse of the kinds of assistance teachers can give their colleagues. With more experienced eyes, she clarified seemingly unsolvable problems for other teachers by moving a few desks, rearranging a few work stations. She provided a vehicle for isolated teachers to share their best ideas; she connected teachers interested in similar kinds of instructional experimentation. In addition, she listened to and validated the struggles of those less familiar with the complexities of teaching. She talked with them about their teaching and offered much-needed reinforcement through her positive comments. Gwen models the kind of support good teachers can provide to one another when they have time to interact. Gwen's frustration at not being able to influence her role in order to bolster its potential offers another valuable lesson in the difficulties of molding a satisfactory teacher leadership position.

All three teachers who held these roles undertook a much broader range of work than is usually suggested in the current discussion about these positions. They engaged in fund raising, peer research on teaching and learning, administrative training, experiential teaching, curriculum development and redesign, leadership training, consulting, collaborative problem solving, instructional diagnosis, and public relations, to mention just a few. They provide solid evidence of the potent resource contained in the classroom teachers of this country. Clearly, these teachers have the energy, the experience, and the intellectual power to address many of the urgent problems in our schools.

BUILDING A DEFINITION OF TEACHER LEADERSHIP

Given the insights gained from Ted, Mary, and Gwen, I feel better able to define what I think teacher leadership should be. In the first chapter, I mentioned the common, generic definition of a leader as someone who has the ability to encourage colleagues to change, to do things they wouldn't ordinarily consider without the influence of the leader. Using that definition of leadership as a starting point, I define teacher leadership as the ability of the teacher leader to engage colleagues in experimentation and then examination of more powerful instructional practices in the service of more engaged student learning. The teacher leaders I visited were interested in a classroom focus, and more specifically in an instructional focus. Many school improvement programs I have worked with engage teachers in the process of determining what would improve their school. One group of teachers chose to recommend that the school be painted. Another instituted a potluck dinner once a month. Mary and Ted were very clear that their overarching goal was to make school a more engaging place for students, and that their time should be spent to that end. They were committed to working with other teachers in order to extend the hope for more rigorous and engaging classrooms. Teacher leadership then means that teachers work with teachers and focus their time and energy on the investigation of challenging instructional strategies.

There is another component to this definition of teacher leadership. All three of these teachers had come to see teaching in a far more complex light as a result of working with colleagues and examining their own practices. As teacher leaders they felt the responsibility to help create a working climate among teachers, which underlined for them the complications posed by the art and science of teaching—the mastery of which extends and develops throughout an entire career. None of them suggested to their colleagues that they—as leaders—had the ultimate approach to teaching. Nor did any of them recommend that all past practices should be discarded in favor of a new approach. Rather, they asked that teachers examine current practices against their hopes for their students, and then suggested additions to existing instructional repertoires. Even Gwen, given that she worked with a prescribed set of instructional strategies, did not suggest that teachers give up practices with which they felt successful but rather encouraged them to consider additional possibilities. The stance taken by the teacher leaders, however, did not mean that they had no standards, that any methods would be fine. Ted and Mary looked constantly to their students for proof of the pudding and attempted to design ways to determine if their techniques were making a difference for kids. As a result, they were involved in a constant process of evaluating and rejecting some of their own past practices, and eliminating those that involved passive learning activities in favor of experiences that required serious student participation.

Mary, Gwen, and Ted offer another important dimension of the definition. Mary and Ted selected the instructional strategies that they believed, based on their working experiences with students, were the most powerful. They did not pick these willy-nilly but selected ones that had available foundations in research and strong undergirding instructional philosophies. Ted first experimented and then determined the foundations that supported his methods. Mary researched first and then experimented. In both cases their selection was based on a rich mixture of theory and practice. Thus they attempted techniques and methods that were based on what Goodlad (1987a) calls an authorized opinion. Gwen was recruited to teach a prescriptive set of teacher behaviors. She did not recommend that a future leadership position stress this particular approach. Because she had not participated in the decision making about the techniques selected, she was less confident in them. The definition of teacher leadership must include some combination of the following empowering responsibilities for teachers:

1. The autonomy to decide which strategies they will work with
2. The freedom to experiment with those techniques with students and with other teachers

3. The opportunity—compulsory—to be engaged in learning about the foundations of the methods they recommend to their colleagues

Finally, an important part of the definition of teacher leadership concerns whether teacher leaders actually teach or not. Mary, Gwen, and Ted all taught. All believed that it enhanced their ability to work with their colleagues. Mary and Ted noted that working with the kids was really the bonus, the incentive, the perk they looked forward to—also an important consideration. In my experience working with a number of teachers in leadership positions, those who spend some portion of their time in the classroom seem more confident about their ability to share real concerns and to collaborate in meaningful ways. I do not believe that all teacher leadership positions require 50% of time in the classroom, nor do I believe that those teacher leaders who don't teach at all have no possibility of influencing their colleagues. I do believe, however, that a critical factor in the serious improvement of instructional practices for students lies in the sharing of actual practice among adults. Teachers have too long been taught by those who have limited awareness of the exigencies of the day-to-day classroom life. Real change in instructional practice requires that both the leaders and their colleagues experiment with methods in classrooms full of kids.

A PROCESS FOR BEGINNING

Ted, Mary, and Gwen made it much clearer to me where I would begin to create or redesign teacher leadership positions. Given the opportunity, I would approach building and implementing a teacher leadership position quite differently than I did 15 years ago. Following is an outline of what I would do in a school that is either beginning to build such opportunities for teachers or redesigning existing positions.

I recommend that administrators and teachers work together through six components to build meaningful teacher leadership positions within their individual school context. Because I am always conscious of budget considerations in schools, I have suggested a sketch of a budget. Funds might come from the school's professional development budget, from a special district allocation, from a one-time grant, or from an allocation from the school's materials budget. I have based my calculations on a secondary school with a certified staff of 80 teachers. With the understanding that each component should be adapted to suit the context of any given school, they are described below:

I. *Teachers and administrators should work collaboratively over the course of a school year to generate several proposals for instructional improvement*, which would include recommendations for leadership positions for teachers to design and implement the proposed programs. Regular and substantial time needs to be scheduled for this collaborative exploration. Each teacher in the building is paid for nine additional hours—one per month—at the district curriculum rate. Nine hours is not much time. To add additional time to the discussion hour, faculty meetings that generally run half an hour every 2 weeks in most schools could be reduced to one meeting of half an hour per month for general school business. This would add half an hour to the monthly discussion time. In order to facilitate these discussions, the staff might be divided into four sections so that groups of 20 teachers and one or two administrators per group could find a mutually convenient hour and a half once a month for their discussions. Each group would elect one teacher to coordinate the discussion. That teacher would be given an extra planning period per day in order to do the following:

1. Coordinate the meeting with staff group.
2. Coordinate with the three other group coordinators before and after each meeting to share results. Major points should be summarized on half a sheet of paper from each of the four monthly meetings and should be made available to the entire faculty.
3. Provide release time by covering classes for any teachers who choose to investigate special topics as a result of their group's discussion.
4. Investigate topics of interest to the discussion group, and provide readings or pertinent articles.
5. Investigate current practices within the discussion group, or gather more personal impressions from individuals in the group and report those back to the whole group in an unbiased manner.
6. Negotiate the use of the five extra hours per week with the

discussion group as they see fit, keeping in mind that the purpose is to assist the discussion group to generate a plan by the end of April for improving the quality of experience that students receive while building more powerful growth opportunities for teachers.
7. Work with the three other coordinators to put all of the groups' suggestions for school improvement into one final report.
8. Design some means of assessing the effectiveness of each of the potential suggestions and the teacher leader's role. The group might suggest a series of questions to be answered by teachers and administrators alike several times during the first year of implementation. Assessment should be considered during the creation of the role rather than after the first year of implementation.

II. *The faculty should engage in a series of focused discussions during the nine small-group sessions as part of their yearlong investigation,* in order to grapple with a number of the issues that proved both problematic and paradoxical in the leadership positions studied. Each of these topics is problematic and sure to evoke strong emotions and reactions. To prepare for this, I suggest that each of the groups generate a series of ground rules that will enable them to engage in frank and open discussions without fear that their opinions or ideas will be circulated among the larger faculty. The ground rules should focus on establishing a climate of mutual trust and respect regardless of differences of opinion. Once the ground rules have been agreed upon by the entire group, the discussions would evolve from the following questions:
1. What are the characteristics of powerful, positive learning experiences?
2. What about our school inhibits or promotes powerful positive learning experiences for students?
3. What kinds of collaborative relationships are available to the adults in the school to reduce isolation and to promote professional growth? Do these relationships improve student learning?
4. What does shared leadership mean to us? How does leadership currently work in our school? What leadership responsibilities do we want? What do we mean by "shared"?

5. Are we willing to learn from our colleagues?
   inside/outside expert syndrome
   professional autonomy versus collaboration
   overt/covert behavior patterns
6. What approaches do we as teachers suggest to promote more powerful learning experiences for students while fostering professional growth for teachers? Would these approaches make schools more personal for kids?
7. How viable are the suggestions we made? What attitudes and assumptions do these suggestions convey about teaching and learning, teachers and students?
8. What incentives are there for the teachers who participate? And for the teachers who take leadership responsibility?
9. How might we select teachers who take leadership responsibility? What is the association's role? Administrator's role?
10. How might we assess whether our suggestions are working to:
    provoke more powerful learning for kids?
    foster professional growth for teachers?

Each of these questions requires that teachers and administrators openly discuss issues that have proved problematic for practicing teacher leaders. Any discussion about how the school should be changed should take as its central purpose the provision of better learning for students. By grappling with this series of questions, participants are asked to think about the conditions that foster powerful learning experiences in general. Each member can look to his or her own experience. The group diagnoses their own school to determine whether the school as it exists fosters these kinds of opportunities for kids. This kind of collaborative diagnosis seldom takes place in schools and should help to sharpen shared beliefs about teaching and learning.

Then, the group investigates current leadership opportunities in the school to determine what kind of impact these positions have on adults and children. A further look at leadership practices in the school should help them to generate some common definitions and some role clarifications. For instance, a group may determine that the department chairs in their school make life much easier for each of the teachers because they take care of the administrative duties aligned with book distribution and the ordering of supplies. On the other hand, these positions do not assist teachers in instructional growth. This clarification may help group members to generate a separate role that focuses on instruction while retaining the department chair positions to facilitate the dissemination of materials. These discussions also might help the group come to a mutual definition of what shared leadership should look like in their school as well as clarify mutual expectations for teacher leadership roles and administrative roles.

In addition, teachers and administrators have opportunity to consider whether they can learn from their colleagues, and if so, in what ways. In these discussions, the groups should begin to generate suggestions for roles and programs that have the potential to improve the educational experiences of students while providing meaningful growth for the adults as well.

In order to troubleshoot, the group analyzes the suggestions made prior to the selection and creation of a position. Any role should have the potential to match its original intentions, and the incentives should be strong enough to encourage meaningful participation.

Although all of these discussions engage people in the collaborative process of creating leadership positions, these last two discussion sessions ask the group to delineate processes for the selection and assessment of the roles suggested. Even though a year may seem a long time to create a simple position or two, my experiences with Ted, Gwen, and Mary lead me to believe that the whole faculty needs to be involved. The seriousness with which people are engaged should help to ensure that the positions have the potential to bring about substantial change. It should also increase the likelihood that both administrators and staff behave overtly rather than covertly. I also believe that the time spent investigating issues related to instructional improvement should foster the kind of climate of inquiry that Sirotnik describes as so central to school improvement (Sirotnik, 1987a,b) and should also promote shared understandings about the nature of teaching and learning among the staff.

III. *The faculty should be asked to assess the benefits of the yearlong discussion.* Several weeks after the discussions had finished, I'd ask staff to do a bit of writing so that we might better understand the impact of the time spent. I might give them prompts like:

1. Describe your reaction to the discussion-group work for the year.
2. Do you believe that the suggestions generated have the potential to improve the professional practice for teachers and provide better learning for students? Why? Why not? Please be as thorough and specific as possible in both your responses.
3. How should we proceed?
4. How would you like to participate?
5. How do you define teacher leadership now?
6. What is shared leadership?
7. What kind of effect did the time spent in the discussion groups have on you as an educator?

IV. *A final report should be prepared that combines the strongest suggestions from the four groups, including processes for selection and evaluation.* The report should also outline the faculty's response to the yearlong investigation. A stipend might be offered to the discussion-group facilitators to prepare and to compile this report or proposal for action to be presented to the staff just before the end of school. The proposal should suggest some alternative possibilities and some decision-making processes.

I would hope to have the final report done prior to the end of the school year so that decisions could be made for the following year. In order to accomplish that, the discussion groups might meet twice during a couple of months to allow the facilitators the time to compile the final reports.

IV. *The budget for such a project might look something like this*:

4 teacher coordinators given one release period per day is equivalent to 2/3 full time; based on an average salary of $32,000 =	$21,333
Stipend of $500 each for the 4 teachers for extra time to prepare the final report =	$ 2,000
80 teachers at 9 hours at $15 per hour =	$10,800
Total Budget	$34,133

VI. *In the last month of school, the faculty should engage in some process suggested by the facilitators for selecting one or two of their options for the next year.* Consensual decision making should be more powerful than a majority vote, as majority votes can leave nearly half of the staff dissatisfied and thus more inclined toward covert resistance. Once the decision has been made, the process for selection and implementation would begin, coupled with the plan to assess the role during the coming year.

Although the agenda suggested in the year of exploration left out any number of possible topics—which instructional strategies foster more powerful learning, how the schedule is organized so that staff have time to work collaboratively, how people go about the process of change—I would hope that the staff would pick up unresolved issues or topics that hadn't had adequate airing.

Then, I would try right along with everyone else not to get too adamant about my personal preference for a particular approach but to be guided by the wisdom of the group. I would, however, have the reassurance that everyone involved had a clearer understanding of the teacher leadership role, its purposes, underlying assumptions, and incentives; that the entire staff was more knowledgeable about our aims in serving kids; and that everyone had the opportunity to participate in the current discussion about teacher leadership.

Once a teacher leadership role created as a result of the suggested process was in place, I, as a teacher and an observer of leadership positions, would want to hang around to watch, listen, and visit with students and teachers to see if attending to the problems and paradoxes that plagued Ted, Gwen, and Mary enabled the teacher leaders to work in more powerful ways. I'd also be curious to see what new problems cropped up in place of those solved.

CONCLUDING IMAGES

The time spent with Mary, Ted, and Gwen was enormously productive for me. It helped me to understand better the practical realities involved in responding to the current national discussion about the need for spirited teacher leadership. It helped me to place the discussion in some sort of history and to hone specific tools to use in the examination of current leadership positions and in the redesign or building of new positions. I felt the way I do every couple of years when I walk out of the optometrist's office after updating my lenses. I see things. Trees have individual leaves instead of green bonnets. Street lights are dots instead of luminescent orbs, and everybody else seems to have developed as many wrinkles as I have.

Last year I spent a couple of weeks in several schools that were new to me. With my improved sight, I was better able to identify the leadership roles teachers were fulfilling. Most of these were new roles, recently designed in schools where teachers and administrators have made a serious commitment to rethinking their educational practices. A couple of schools had developed leadership positions that required leaders to undertake an administrative focus. In one case, the teacher leader had been designated by the principal, and the two of them had hashed out the responsibilities for the role. That teacher leader ended up playing the role of the administrator for the team—revising schedules, talking to parents, setting meeting agendas.

In another school, four teachers shared 100 students. Each teacher taught one of the core subjects—math, history, science, or English. These teachers had a cooperative planning period each day and met regularly during that period. In their meetings they checked their students' progress, shared suggestions for working with problem students, and loosely coordinated their curriculum. When the history teacher taught the Greeks, the English teacher had the students read a Greek tragedy, while the math teacher prepared lessons on the development of geometry. During the time they worked together, it appeared that their mutual planning time influenced when they would each cover what parts of the curriculum, but not how they taught. There was little discussion of the actual method of instruction.

The group had agreed that each teacher would coordinate those meetings one week per month. As the COW—coordinator of the week—the leader was responsible for serving as the liaison between the administration and the team and ensuring that everyone brought important issues to the table. Again, the work these leaders did was important and of great assistance to their team's work in rethinking educational practices.

Another school was particularly riveting in that the teacher leader seemed to function in a role that was focused on instructional change. Evelyn had been teaching for some 18 years in large urban high schools. She was used to the hectic pace of high schools, the constant interruptions, and the terrific need to keep track of the kids.

In order to do the kind of in-depth work with students she believed was necessary, she had moved to a smaller, more innovative school within the large city system. In her current job, she taught humanities to ninth- and tenth-grade students. Students in this school were double age-grouped and worked in classes that were interdisciplinary and 2 hours long. Evelyn taught one humanities block, had a 1-hour daily meeting with her advisory group—a small group of students she worked with in an advisor/advisee capacity—and then filled a teacher leadership role for the remainder of the day. Her title was team leader, and she fenced anything and everything that had to do with curriculum and instruction for the seven teachers who taught the ninth/tenth-grade humanities block. She worked with newcomers to the school on a regular basis as they switched from subject-area specialists with 50-minute classes to subject-area generalists with 2-hour classes. She worked over their lesson plans with them, watched them teach, modeled lessons when they needed to see someone else do it. She organized people to cover their courses so they could watch her.

She dropped in on everyone's classes and prompted people to try things they were skeptical of, encouraging them that it would be okay if a tactic flopped, that they would simply learn a few things and move on. One of her colleagues, Kathryn, was afraid to move from teacher-centered to student-centered instruction. Evelyn coaxed her and helped her to see how she might do the same lesson with greater student involvement. Kathryn told me that it was now embarrassing for her to look back on her fears, and she acknowledged the benefit of Evelyn's prompting. In addition, Evelyn facilitated the 4-hour meetings the team had each week to work together. "I think this is the most important aspect of the changes we made in the school. It enabled the teachers to reach consensus about what should be taught and how. We had to talk everything over. We've argued and struggled and polarized, but in the long run, we've all learned a lot about both teaching and learning."

I sat in on one of these meetings. Evelyn had an agenda—schedules and details first. Then she passed out short stories written by Caribbean authors that one of the teachers had located. They wanted these stories so they could provide more examples of work done by authors who reflected the cultural and racial heritage of their students. Evelyn had gone to two libraries to find copies of the recommended stories, then organized the photocopying and collating. She stapled them herself, as their school—like most schools—was short of help. That accomplished, the bulk of the meeting was spent on a discussion about how they might best measure what kinds of knowledge and skills students had gained in a yearlong course of study on the topic "What Is Justice?" As I listened, I felt jubilant and depressed: depressed because it was this kind of intellectual exchange between the adults in my school that I longed for but never found; jubilant because this group of teachers was tackling the most difficult problems that face education today. How do we get students engaged? How do we give them the kinds of skills that will help them to participate in the real world? How will we know when they know?

She moved the discussion back and forth between consideration of the measures they should use and the course outline that they had collaboratively developed. "Where do we have interactive lessons where the kids get practice and feedback doing that—taking different perspectives?" Everyone in the group felt strongly about what should be taught, when it should be taught, and in what manner. After a difficult, racially hot debate between two teachers who disputed the appropriateness of a particular film about South Africa as a teaching tool, she asked the two contenders to generate several acceptable solutions to their disagreement to present to the group in a special meeting to be held later in the week, and rounded the troops back up around the central issue of the day—how were they to measure whether the kids really understood what justice is? Eventually, they agreed that they had a draft of several performance assessments, which she would prepare for their future scrutiny.

At the end of the session, she reserved a few minutes to say, "Okay, folks. What do you want me to do for you in the next couple of weeks? Did I screw up on anything? Have I forgotten anything of importance?" Without hesitation, they let her know. Had she ordered the books for their next 2-week unit? Would she come into a class where one of the teachers was practicing a debate? On Tuesday, could she cover a class so that one of the teachers could watch one of the other teachers conduct a Socratic seminar? Did she have any articles on Socratic questioning?

I rolled the requests and her actions around in my mind. In some cases, she was mentoring. In others, she suggested a division of labor, but her work was around getting instructional materials together and experimenting with additional instructional techniques—completely focused on the classroom and on students. The whole team was in a partnering relationship as they collaborated to come to consensus about what they would teach and how. The teachers were able to shape their individual interactions with her as well as participate in the decision making about their collective focus. Their efforts were squarely on what the kids would be doing in the classroom. The teachers critiqued her work on a regular basis—every week, and then more rigorously at the end of the year for revisions in the role for the next year.

> The most important thing that we do is to figure out how to work better each week and every year for the kids. The harder we work to engage the kids, the more we get from them in return, the more worthwhile all of our haggling and niggling is, and the more worth-while all those hours spent working together—which sometimes, oftentimes seems like they are going nowhere—are. The teachers in our school are really good now at figuring out what we need to change in order to give more to the kids. It's been a great experience for me. I have learned so much from them, and every year I recognize what small steps we've taken and how much further we have to go. I'm glad to help, to be a part of it.

I left this school feeling a burst of energy. Ted, Mary, and Gwen had taught me what to look for in teacher leadership, and what to be wary of. As I reflect on all that I have learned, I believe that teacher leadership positions like Evelyn's, Ted's, and Mary's will make a difference in the quality of educational experiences students receive and in the quality of working life adults experience in schools. I believe that positions like Gwen's help us to see that the roles must be carefully designed and implemented so that they have the potential to make a difference. The images I come away with convince me that teachers in this country have the expertise, the problem-solving abilities, and the diverse skills needed to lead their colleagues and their students into more powerful schools. They need only the opportunity for real and meaningful participation.

APPENDIX

The Methodology

Because there is limited work done on teacher leadership and growing interest, the methodology used for this study may prove helpful
to those who wish to add to the small body of research accumulated
thus far. In addition, it will allow those with expertise the means to
better determine the validity of the assertions made.

PILOT-STUDY RESEARCH

Before undertaking the study for this book, I did a pilot study that
significantly influenced the design of this study. Briefly, I observed
seven teachers over a period of seven months. All were selected
for their positions by their administrators. Three were on full-time
release to fulfill their leadership responsibilities, whereas four others
maintained some or full-time teaching responsibility. The intention of
the study was to determine whether these roles improved the flat
nature of the teaching career, to determine whether teachers in
extended positions felt more successful if they maintained some classroom responsibility, and whether these positions decreased teacher
isolation. The unit of analysis was the interaction each teacher leader
had with fellow teachers, students, or administrators.

Findings from this study reinforced the survey research done by
Hatfield et al. (1987) and the case-study research done by Porter
(1986): Those who hold extended positions benefit enormously from
the opportunity to engage in new kinds of work. I found that those
who maintained classroom responsibility believed they had greater
credibility with their teaching colleagues than those on full-time
release. It was difficult for me to confirm this because no information
was collected from their colleagues to support these beliefs. For the

same reason, it was difficult to determine whether these roles improved the lives of those teachers they were designed to serve.

The roles did appear to be vague and dependent on administrative prerogative. In addition, teachers who were on full-time release were not supported by their teacher associations because their positions were believed to increase the class loads of the other teachers. Further, there was scant evidence of teacher-to-teacher work. Although most of the roles were described as support for curriculum and instruction, most of the work was in fact administrative in nature. Throughout the duration of my observations, colleagues at the schools where I was observing pulled me aside to air their concerns that these positions were miniadministrator roles.

This study clearly led me to include interviews with teacher leaders' colleagues, to check the position of the local association, and to ask again whether classroom experience was important to personal credibility. Furthermore, because the variation in the context of each of these roles so significantly shaped the role, I was spurred on to reduce the number of cases so that I could examine the context and its influence on the roles more closely.

CASE-STUDY RESEARCH

I chose to do a multiple case study of three teachers who hold leadership positions of different kinds in various parts of the country. The study was exploratory in nature in order to begin to generate some understanding of the complexity of these roles and the way they fit into their surrounding culture.

I chose to do case studies for a variety of reasons. The research that existed when I began this study consisted of two fairly extensive survey research data bases (Hatfield et al., 1987; Dierks et al., 1988) and several exploratory sets of case studies (see Porter, 1986; Lieberman, Saxl, & Miles, 1988; Wasley, 1987). Together, these studies pried the lock off Pandora's box but left much of the contents unexplored. The questions that emerged required descriptive kinds of data in order fully to uncover the complexity of the roles.

Furthermore, I was interested in gathering interpretive data that would help to clarify the importance of the cultural context in which these leadership roles exist. My interest here was influenced by the work of Sarason (1971) and Geertz (1973). By engaging in case studies, I had the opportunity to document the complex interaction between teacher leaders and their surrounding circumstances—terrifying complexity and all.

In addition, I have been strongly influenced by those around me who continue to argue that research must lie closer to the heart of actual practice if we are to have any possibility of reforming schools (see, e.g., Lieberman, 1988b; Goodlad, 1987a,b; Sirotnik, 1987a). Experience has convinced them, and me, that research is too often conducted by outsiders who have little understanding of the day-to-day complexities of school life, and who, as a result, generate findings that do not ring true to practitioners in schools. Teachers, policymakers, and researchers alike have long been irritated by their inability to match purposes so that what is done by one is of use to the others (see Schulman, 1983; Sarason, 1971; Berman & McLaughlin, 1978).

Geertz (1973) reinforces the need to look toward practice. "If you want to understand what a science is, you should look in the first instance, not at its theories or its findings, and certainly not at what its apologists say about it; you should look at what the practitioners of it do" (p. 5). By selecting case-study methodology, then, I hoped to gather data on the complexity of daily practice and to check my perceptions with the subjects in the hope that we might come a little closer to data that teachers themselves would have generated if they had engaged in the research process, and that they would find accurately descriptive of their own practice. By spending time with individual teachers and recording their circumstances, and by interviewing their colleagues, it was my hope that the data might better reflect the actual voices of a very small sample of teachers.

Case-study methodology also filled some of my personal requisites based on my own experience as both a high school and an elementary teacher and as someone who has worked closely with teachers for the last 15 years. Teaching is, for adults, working alone. As noted in the review of the literature, teachers spend the majority of their time behind classroom doors without the benefit of discussion with their colleagues. It is a nonreflective profession, in that the day is very full from the moment teachers park to the minute they back out: kids swirling around with 100 different questions, needs, personal stories to tell; mailboxes full of literature that needs sorting, reading, trashing; forms that need filling out, filing, returning; committees to sit on, conferences to schedule; phone calls to make to parents; field trips to organize, evaluation conferences with principals, not to mention lessons to prepare—and then run off on obsolete ditto machines that move more slowly than a cautious tortoise. Teaching simply is not designed to support thoughtful reflection about practice or conversations among adults that would promote professional growth.

I wanted to conduct research that possibly would allow the participants the opportunity to reflect—to converse with another adult concerned about the work of teachers—that would provide a kind of intellectual stimulation for which so many teachers long. Case-study research allowed me to spend 2 weeks with each of the subjects, so we had large chunks of time to discuss and to reflect on teacher leadership, their particular insights into these positions, and the improvement of professional practice.

On a more practical note, case-study methodology allowed me to gather qualitative data without investing the length of time required in a full-blown ethnography.

As a result of these influences and this reasoning, I was able to record the daily experience of a few teachers in leadership positions in the midst of their working context. The methodology allowed me to extend the knowledge of the cultural context to collect data closer to the heart of teaching and to double-check my field notes with my subjects to ensure that the notes reflected descriptions of their practice that they considered accurate. In addition, by including interviews with colleagues in the case studies, I was able to give brief voice to those who are supposed to be the recipients of the benefits of these leadership roles.

Dealing with Bias

Case-study methodology, along with other qualitative methods, is based upon perceptual recording of information and on the perceptual analysis of that information. Those engaged in it are frequently accused of defending their own positions and of gathering only data that support their initial positions. An attempt was made to build this study in such a way that bias would be minimized. In data collection, analysis, and reporting procedures, systematic cross checks were devised.

In data collection procedures, I attempted to protect against bias by beginning the study without preconceived notions about the findings. Although I did have particular questions, the answers to those questions would necessarily emerge from the data. Multiple data sources were used—interviews, observations, interviews with colleagues, and pertinent documentation collected at each site. During data collection, I reviewed my field notes each evening, so that confusing information might be clarified and contradictory information pursued.

In addition, the interview instruments were field tested and submitted to the subjects of this study for second-round clarification. Finally, observational data were recorded continually rather than selectively. Although this generated a great deal of data, I felt more confident that the information was not extracted selectively.

When I was analyzing the data, triangulation constituted a major activity—both within the individual cases and across the cases. The dominant themes that are described at the end of each case are the result of triangulated data.

As another means by which to check bias, each of the cases was submitted to the subject for his or her comments, so that the subjects could ensure that their working circumstances had been accurately portrayed. Each of the subjects had another colleague in his or her school read the piece to determine its accuracy from a third perspective.

In all cases, I tried to allow the accumulated information to speak for itself—including direct quotations from interviews, from the field notes, and from the transcribed tapes—rather than reporting it interpretatively. Exact notations of the data source are included in my dissertation referenced in the acknowledgments.

Study Sample

The sample for the study consisted of three teachers: Ted Newton, Mary Jones, and Gwen Ingman. All came from National Education Association states and were members of that organization and the state affiliate. All were selected because they represented a different segment of the teaching population and because they held different kinds of leadership roles within their teaching community.

Ted had been teaching for 22 years at the high school level in a rural eastern community and has achieved national recognition for his work with students. The successful nature of his projects with students has allowed him to form a sort of school within a school and to form an outside corporation that he runs. As a result, he teaches four classes per day in the local high school where he is the senior staff person. The rest of his time is spent running the corporation, which involves hiring other teachers who teach according to his philosophy, also in the regular local high school. He works with a board of directors, obtains funding from outside sources, and oversees a large budget that supports a variety of activities. In an attempt to spread his very successful teaching philosophy, he teaches college courses in many different states and has a support staff that coordinates teacher outreach networks for those teachers who wish to experiment with his methodology after taking the course.

However, he held no formal leadership role within his own school district. Ted was selected for this study because his position is self-created and provides enormous leadership for teachers around the country, while he functions as a regular—though entrepreneurial—teacher within his own system. I gained permission to study Ted by writing to him with an accompanying recommendation from Ann Lieberman, who served on his board of directors. We communicated through letters for a period of a year and a half in order to make the circumstances of the study clear. Ted participated in the study with some reticence, as he did not consider himself to be a teacher leader.

I located Mary by asking both administrators and highly respected teachers within the district who would be a good subject for this particular study, and then contacted her by phone. She was pleased to participate. Mary has been teaching middle school students for 30 years. She teaches in a western suburban school district that is experiencing the shift from suburban affluence to urban complexity. Mary originally applied for and was hired as a teacher on special assignment, a formal leadership position created in her district. In that position, her responsibility was to provide instructional support for teachers (hence, IST) to help them to experiment with new methodologies.

After 4 years, Mary did not believe that her position was working particularly well. Other teachers did not take advantage of the IST's expertise, or when they did invite Mary into their classrooms to work, they often used it as catchup time rather than as professional development time. As a result, she and a fellow specialist designed an

experimental project where they would team-teach 60 heterogeneously mixed students, using a variety of instructional techniques and
an integrated approach to curriculum. The classroom was to be a
demonstration center for other teachers—a place where they could
come to observe and to experiment themselves. Mary also did in-
service presentations for other teachers within her district and
taught a variety of courses. Her case was particularly interesting
because she had held a leadership role that she perceived did not
work well, and so exercised some leadership in creating another
model. The district fully supported her efforts.

Gwen's case was interesting because there were rumors afloat
that the position was not supported by the teachers. I had worked
with Gwen for a period of a year through the advisory board of a
teacher leadership project where she represented her district. To
investigate working with her, I called administrators and several
other teachers for recommendations and then contacted her in person. She was also eager to participate. Gwen taught in a rural
elementary school and was just finishing her 10th year. She had been
appointed to a half-time specialist position in order to support other
teachers in their practice of Madeline Hunter's approach to teaching,
Instructional Theory into Practice (ITIP). Gwen's position was formal, inspired by the superintendent, and then instituted by the
central office at the ratio of one teacher specialist per building. A
teaching librarian in the morning, she visited other teachers' classrooms in the afternoon in order to observe and demonstrate for them
such techniques as teaching to objectives, anticipatory set, monitoring, adjusting, or reteaching.

This position was designed to support better instruction and to
provide teachers with greater collegial opportunities. She also taught
a college course in ITIP once during the year for teachers throughout
the district. These positions had been subject to some controversy
when instituted 3 years earlier, but were reported by administrators
and by several of the teachers who held the positions to be very
successful and well supported when I undertook this study.

Colleague Interviews

In order to gather data from the teachers who worked with the
teacher leaders, interviews were conducted with four people at two of

the sites and, because of the unavailability of one of the interviewees, three at Mary's site. These interviews were held to gather information on whether teacher leaders needed to maintain classroom responsibility in order to retain credibility, to explore whether the leadership roles that existed in their schools affected the quality of their professional lives, whether the roles were efficacious, and what other teachers would create given the opportunity to devise a leadership role that would support better teaching.

The interviewed teachers were selected to be representative of a wide variety of attitudes from within the teaching staff. I asked each of the subjects to help me identify one staff member who really believed in and supported the work the leader was doing, someone who was neutral, someone who did not support the work, and the union representative in each school. Rather than surveying all of the teachers to determine general attitudes toward these positions, I was more interested in determining the range of attitudes so that I might have a better idea of what these leaders actually had to contend with when dealing with their colleagues. Each of the interviewees was contacted during the first week that I was in the school. Interviews were conducted during the second week.

Propositions and Questions

Protocols for the study were developed in early February 1988. They outlined the major proposition under consideration: Teacher leadership roles that currently exist in school systems are a storehouse of information about leadership roles for teachers. Through examination of these roles, we can determine how to strengthen the opportunities that are available to teachers in order to attract and retain excellent teachers while simultaneously improving the quality of the educational experience for young people. From this central proposition, a guiding question emerged: What is the nature of teacher leadership as it currently exists in schools today? The subquestions that I believed would illuminate the larger question were also clarified. These questions for teacher leaders, used in the conduct of a lengthy interview, were:

1. What is the nature of the work you do as a lead teacher?
2. What are the constraints of your position?

3. What conditions support your position?
4. How do you define teacher leadership?
5. How were you selected for a leadership position?
6. What kind of leadership roles would be most helpful in improving the quality of education for our young people?
7. Does the association support your position?
8. Do teachers with leadership positions have greater peer support if they maintain some classroom responsibility?
9. Does your extended role add to or detract from teaching?
10. Does your role improve the flat nature of the teaching career?
11. Does it reduce the traditional isolation in which teachers work?

Questions for the subject's colleagues were also used in interviews:

1. What does teacher leadership mean to you?
2. What kinds of leadership opportunities exist for teachers in your school district, your building?
3. In your opinion, are the leadership positions in your building supported by the teacher's association? By your district?
4. What kinds of leadership opportunities would you like to see in place?
5. How should teachers be selected for these roles? Evaluated?
6. Does the subject provide leadership for you and the other teachers in your building?

Protocols were sent to and discussed with the subjects at the beginning of my time with them. In all three cases they were invited to revise the questions under consideration. The questionnaire for the colleague interview was revised by Ted Smith at the outset of the study and was then used with all other groups.

Data Collection

Data collection was done during two consecutive weeks with each participant. I spent the bulk of the working day with the teacher leaders and recorded both formal, scheduled time and informal, break time. Where possible, I attended evening meetings and class sessions conducted by the teachers. In addition, I visited several classrooms of teachers who were to be the recipients of the leader's assistance.

I recorded handwritten field notes throughout the day at each of the sites. In addition to the recorded observations kept throughout my stay in each place, I conducted extensive interviews with both the subjects and with four of their colleagues.

The interviews with the subjects were based on the questions listed above. In all cases the teachers were asked to preview the questions and to add any they believed would be pertinent to the study. Ted made the only revisions. The initial interview took approximately 2 hours per subject and was tape-recorded. Transcriptions of those tapes are available as part of the data corpus. After the initial interview, subsequent interviews were conducted in order to check perceptions collected during data gathering and to extend information obtained during the initial interview. Some of these interviews were handwritten rather than recorded.

Colleague interviews were conducted during the course of the 2 weeks at each site, most often during the interviewee's planning period. In one case, the teacher leader offered to cover the classes of those to be interviewed, because it seemed to her helpful and part of her job and because the other teachers were unwilling to give up their time in order to be interviewed. I was initially concerned that this circumstance might skew their responses, but that concern disappeared during the course of the interviews. These interviews were handwritten by me and lasted from 20 minutes to an hour and a half.

In addition, I kept a field journal, recording my own personal observations and checking my own biases during the progress of the study. The field journal focused mainly on the unforeseen difficulties encountered in establishing rapport with subjects and the progress of those relationships.

At each site, artifacts were collected—memos, curriculum guides, course outlines, student papers, books, magazines, articles—anything that contributed to an understanding of the teacher leader's work or context. Each item was verified with the teacher leader and is available for review.

Data Analysis

Data analysis procedures were influenced by Yin's (1984) description of individual case and cross-case analysis, by Erickson's

(1986) description of tracing the evidentiary warrant, and by Light-foot's (1983) descriptions of portraiture. I had two primary objectives in mind when I began data analysis. In order to check the validity of the original study proposition, it seemed necessary for me to be able to describe two things.

First, I wanted to detail the complexity of the actual roles within their contexts. I wanted to create a picture for each one so that readers could begin to see how and where these people work.

Second, I wanted to analyze the data for answers to the questions that had framed the study. Therefore, data analysis took place in three distinct parts. The first was for general familiarity with the entire data corpus; the second involved assembling information for the portraits; the third included processes for locating answers to the questions. Because this was an exploratory study, it contained embedded units of analysis—the subjects themselves, the collegial interviews, and the contexts—that provided the focus for each stage of the analysis. So, in each stage of the three-part process, I searched for defensible information within each of the units of analysis. In order to establish a reasonable evidentiary warrant, I developed a coding procedure that would allow the reader to trace any assertions made back to the data corpus itself.

I began data analysis by reading through the entire corpus three times for general impressions, and then for the beginnings of deeper understandings. The data corpus consisted of 700 pages of field notes plus another 35 pages of tape transcriptions. The document collection was huge and included 17 books. Although I read several of the books completely, I skimmed a number because I was already familiar with them. I took notes during each of these readings in order to track my impressions as I became more familiar with the data.

The second round of analysis involved rereading each set of field notes from the three subjects to compile information for portraits or descriptions of practice. I began by identifying each of the interactions that I observed in categories that outlined the nature of the work—teacher-to-teacher work, administrative work, mentoring work, personal business, and staff socializing. Each incident I recorded during the course of the 2 weeks of observation with each subject was categorized in this way. For instance, Ted's interactions fell under the following categories: (1) teaching students, (2) administrative work for Talking Mountain, (3) teacher outreach work,

(4) fund-raising, (5) mentoring staff members, and (6) staff social-izing. Each of the subject's work fell into different categories.

As is to be expected, data analysis becomes a process of explora-tion and gathering understandings as one goes. At this point in the analysis—after creating the portraits of daily life—it became more and more apparent to me that I needed to trace the contextual features of each study more specifically, more overtly. It was impor-tant to me to demonstrate how each case was influenced by the context in which each of the subjects worked. In order to do that, I went back through each case and compiled pertinent information that emerged during the course of the study that would explain the context.

In addition, it became more and more apparent to me that the personal characteristics, the personal histories, and the philosophies of each of the subjects influenced the leadership role and the per-sonal definition of teacher leadership. Thus, I again perused the data from each case to compile a sketch of the subjects that might help the reader to get a closer sense of the actual person. These two additional bits of analysis became the introductory sections to the portraits included in the next chapter. Occasionally, during this stage, I would clarify categories; as a result, I found myself moving backward and forward between considerations of context, person, and types of work.

Next, I analyzed colleague interviews for each case by listing the range of responses for each question, and then by looking for catego-ries within the responses.

The third and final round of analysis involved lengthy cross-case analysis. I began by using simple critical-thinking techniques—generating similarities between the cases, listing differences. Parker, in a recent paper written with Mueller and Wendling (1989), calls this process "crisscrossing in the search mode," a term that delighted me because it so accurately describes the process I used. For instance, each case led me to certain propositions, such as, "All of the teacher leaders engage in mentoring." I then moved back and forth between the cases and the various relationships within the cases to ensure that such assumptions were correct. Establishing clear-cut differences between the cases was the easiest task in this process.

The cross-case analysis was more complex as I looked for sim-ilarities. Although there were many similarities—each of the subjects was involved in collegial relationships, for example—all of them were contextually bound. The discovery of similarities led me back then to the differences. In order to check the data for similarities, I retraced the evidence from within the data corpus to make sure that my assumptions could be supported. Because each of the cases was unique, it was difficult to find any assertions that held true for all three.

Coding the Data Sources

Five data sources were used in order to present the interactions and circumstances as close to the way I experienced them as possible. They are:

1. Interviews with the subjects
2. Colleague interviews
3. Field notes
4. Documents collected at each site
5. Personal conversations with the subjects

The individual source is identified in the original work after each situation so that the evidence can easily be traced back to the source. The coding to these sources was as follows: Ted is subject 1; Gwen is subject 2; Mary is subject 3. References from the field notes are indicated as (FN, Subj 1, p. 2). Subject interviews are indicated as (Subj 2, Int. p. 6). Colleague interviews are indicated as: (CI, Subj 1, Int. 1, 2, 3, or 4) to identify the subject and the colleague interview. Documents are indicated as: (Subj 1, Doc 19). Personal conversations are indicated as: (Prsnl conv., Subj 2, December 3, 1988).

Negotiating Meanings

The three major subjects of this study had access to a draft of their cases and the findings prior to its completion. They reviewed each of their cases after the initial draft was written and submitted suggestions to tighten the accuracy of the cases. In addition, at least one of their colleagues read the draft to check for accuracy. Factual errors were, of course, corrected. Changes that involved differences between our perceptions were negotiated between the subject and me, as we worked to come to shared understandings. Records of the suggested changes are available as part of the data corpus. This was a difficult process, because not all of the findings were complimentary or pleasant. There were moments when I felt that my observations as an outsider were less encumbered than theirs, and moments when the subjects believed that the limited amount of time I spent with them caused me to be shortsighted and/or shallow. By negotiating, I believe that we came closer to accuracy.

References

Bacharach, S. B. (1986). *The learning workplace: The conditions and resources of teaching.* Washington, DC: National Education Association.

Bass, B. M. (Ed.). (1981). *Stogdill's handbook of leadership: A survey of theory and research* (Rev. and expanded ed.). New York: Free Press.

Berman, D., & McLaughlin, M. W. (1978). *Federal programs supporting educational change, Vol. VIII: Implementing and sustaining innovations.* Santa Monica, CA: Rand Corporation.

Boyer, E. L. (1983). *High school.* New York: Harper and Row.

Carnegie Foundation for the Advancement of Teaching (1986). *A nation prepared: Teachers for the 21st century* (Report of the Task Force on Teaching as a Profession). New York: Author.

Clark, D. (1987). *Thinking about leaders and followers: Restructuring the roles of principals and teachers.* Paper presented at the Restructuring Schooling for Quality Education Conference, Trinity University, San Antonio, TX.

Cohn, M., Kottkamp, R. B., McCloskey, G. N., & Provenzo, E. F. (1987). *Teachers' perspectives on the problems in their profession: Implications for policymakers and practitioners* (Report prepared for the Office of Educational Research and Improvement). Washington, DC: United States Department of Education.

Cuban, L. (1988). A fundamental puzzle of school reform. *Phi Delta Kappan, 69*(5), 340-344.

Darling-Hammond, L. (1984). *Beyond the commission reports: The coming crisis in teaching.* Santa Monica, CA: Rand Corporation.

Darling-Hammond, L. (1988). *Teacher professionalism: Why and how?* Paper written for the New York Task Force on Professionalism.

Devaney, K. (1987). *The lead teacher.* Paper prepared for the Task Force on Teaching as a Profession, Carnegie Forum on Education and the Economy.

Dierks, K., Dillard, S., McElliot, K., Morgan, J., Schultz, B., Tipps, L., & Wallentine, K. (1988). *Teacher leadership: Commitment and challenge* (Research report). Seattle: University of Washington, Puget Sound Educational Consortium.

Erickson, F. (1986). Qualitative methods on research in teaching. In M. Wittrock (Ed.), *Handbook of research on teaching* (3rd ed., pp. 3-36). New York: Macmillan.

Fay, C. (1990, April). *Teaching and leading: In the teacher's voice.* Paper presented at the American Educational Research Association Annual Meeting, Boston.

Finn, C. (1985). Teacher unions and school quality: Potential allies or inevitable foes?

In J. Bunzel (Ed.), *Challenge to American schools: The case for standards and values* (pp. 99-124). New York: Oxford University Press.

Geertz, C. (1973). *The interpretation of cultures.* New York: Basic Books.

Goodlad, J. I. (1984). *A place called school.* New York: McGraw Hill.

Goodlad, J. I. (Ed.). (1987a). *The ecology of school improvement.* Chicago: University of Chicago Press.

Goodlad, J. I. (1987b). *Linking schools and universities: Symbolic partnerships* (Occasional Paper No. 1, pp. 1-44). Seattle: University of Washington, Center for Educational Renewal.

Hatfield, R. C., Blackman, C., Claypool, C., & Master, F. (1987). *Extended professional roles of teacher leaders in the public schools.* Unpublished paper, Michigan State University, East Lansing.

Holmes Group. (1986). *Tomorrow's teachers: A report of the Holmes Group.* East Lansing, MI: Author.

Hunter, M. (1976). *Improved instruction.* El Segundo, CA: TIP Publications.

Kerr, D. H. (1987). *Authority and responsibility in public schooling* (NSSE Yearbook). Chicago: University of Chicago Press.

Lambert, L. (1988). Staff development redesigned. *Phi Delta Kappan, 69*(9), 665-668.

Lieberman, A. (1985-86). *A case study: Parkside school: She is a saint everywhere* (Consortium Evaluation Report). New York: New York City Teacher Center.

Lieberman, A. (1986). Collaborative research: Working with, not working on. *Educational Leadership, 43*(5), 28-32.

Lieberman, A. (1988a). Expanding the leadership team. *Educational Leadership, 45*(5), 4-8.

Lieberman, A. (1988b). Teachers and principals: Turf, tension, and new tasks. *Phi Delta Kappan, 69*(9), 648-653.

Lieberman, A. (1988c). *Building an ecumenical view.* Unpublished paper.

Lieberman, A., & Miller, L. (1984). *Teachers: Their world and their work: Implications for school improvement.* Alexandria, VA: Association for Supervision and Curriculum Development.

Lieberman, A., & Rosenholtz, S. (1987). *The road to school improvement: Barriers and bridges.* Chicago: University of Chicago Press.

Lieberman, A., Saxl, E. R., & Miles, M. B. (1988). Teacher leadership: Ideology and practice. In A. Lieberman (Ed.), *Building a professional culture in schools* (pp. 148-166). New York: Teachers College Press.

Lightfoot, S. L. (1983). *The good high school.* New York: Basic Books.

Little, J. W. (1986). Seductive images and organizational realities in professional development. In A. Lieberman (Ed.), *Rethinking school improvement* (pp. 26-44). New York: Teachers College Press.

Little, J. W. (1988). Assessing the prospects for teacher leadership. In A. Lieberman (Ed.), *Building a professional culture in schools* (pp. 78-106). New York: Teachers College Press.

Livingston, C. (1991). *Windows on teacher leadership.* Washington, DC: National Education Association.

Lortie, D. C. (1969). The balance of control and autonomy in elementary school teaching. In A. Etzioni (Ed.), *The semi-professions and their organizations* (pp. 1-53). New York: Free Press.

Lortie, D. C. (1975). *School teachers*. Chicago: University of Chicago Press.

McCloskey, G., Porvenzo, E. F., Cohen, M., & Kottkamp, R. B. (1987). *A profession at risk: Legislated learning as a disincentive to teaching* (Contract #ERI-P-86-3088). Washington, DC: Office of Educational Research and Improvement, U.S. Department of Education.

McLaughlin, M. W., Wallin, R., Pfeifer, S., Swanson-Owens, D., & Yee, S. M. (1986). Why teachers won't teach. *Phi Delta Kappan, 67*(6), 420-426.

McLaughlin, M. W., & Yee, S. M. (1988). School as a place to have a career. In A. Lieberman (Ed.), *Building a professional culture in schools* (pp. 23-44). New York: Teachers College Press.

McNeil, L. M. (1986). *Contradictions of control: School structure and school knowledge*. New York: Routledge and Kegan Paul.

Meyer, M. S. (1971). *Every employee a manager*. New York: McGraw Hill.

Miller, L. (1990, April). *The emergence of teacher leadership through inquiry*. Paper presented at the American Educational Reform Association Annual Meeting, Boston.

Parker, W., Mueller, M., & Wendling, L. (1989). Critical reasoning on civic issues. *Theory and Research in Social Education, 17*(1), 7-32.

Popkewitz, T., Tabachnick, B., & Wehlage, G. (1982). *The myth of educational reform: A study of school responses to a program of change*. Madison: University of Wisconsin Press.

Porter, A. (1986). Teacher collaboration: New partnership to attack old problems. *Phi Delta Kappan, 69*(2), 147-152.

Rosenholtz, S. (1989). *Teachers' workplace: The social organization of schools*. New York: Longman.

Sarason, S. B. (1971). *The culture of the school and the problem of change*. Boston: Allyn and Bacon.

Sarason, S. B. (1972). *The creation of settings and the future societies*. San Francisco: Jossey-Bass.

Shulman, L. S. (1983). Autonomy and obligation: The remote control of teaching. In L. S. Shulman & G. Sykes (Eds.), *Handbook of teaching and policy* (pp. 484-504). New York: Longman.

Shulman, L. S. (1987). Knowledge and teaching: Foundations of the new reform. *Harvard Educational Review, 57*(1), 1-22.

Sirotnik, K. A. (1987a). *The school as the center of change*. Paper presented at the Southwestern Bell Invitational Conference on Restructuring Schooling for Quality Education: A Reform Agenda, Trinity University, San Antonio, TX.

Sirotnik, K. A. (1987b). *Evaluation in the ecology of schooling: The process of school renewal*. Chicago: University of Chicago Press.

Sizer, T. R. (1984). *Horace's compromise: The dilemma of the American high school*. Boston: Houghton Mifflin.

Soder, R. (1986). *Professionalizing the profession: Notes on the future of teaching*

(Occasional Paper No. 4). Seattle: University of Washington, Center for Educational Renewal.

Smylie, M., & Denny, J. (1989, March). *Lead teachers: Ambiguities and tensions in organizational perspective.* Paper presented at the American Educational Research Association Annual Meeting, San Francisco.

Sykes, G. (1983). Public policy and the problem of teacher quality: The need for screens and magnets. *Handbook of teaching and policy.* New York: Longman.

Sykes, G. (1987). Reckoning with the spectre of professionalism. *Educational Researcher, 16*(6), 19-21.

Theobold, N. (1987). *Who will teach our children?* Report to the Office of the Superintendent of Public Instruction, Olympia, WA.

Waller, W. (1961). *The sociology of teaching.* New York: Russell and Russell.

Wasley, P. A. (1987). *From crisis to restructuring: A study of teachers in lead positions.* Unpublished paper.

Wasley, P. A. (1988). *Teacher leadership and the NEA.* Unpublished paper.

Wasley, P. A. (1989). *The Rhetoric of Reform and the Realities of Practice: A study of lead teachers.* Unpublished doctoral dissertation, University of Washington, Seattle.

Wasley, P. A. (1991). Working together: Teacher leadership and collaboration. In C. Livingston (Ed.), *Windows on teacher leadership.* Washington, DC: National Education Association.

Wise, A. E. (1979). *Legislated learning.* Berkeley: University of California Press.

Wise, A. E. (1988). Legislated learning revisited. *Phi Delta Kappan, 69*(5), 328-332.

Yin, R. K. (1984). *Case study research: Design and methods.* Beverly Hills: Sage Publications.

Selected Bibliography

Cole, S. (1969). *The unionization of teachers.* New York: Praeger.

Cooper, M. (1988). Whose culture is it, anyway? In A. Lieberman (Ed.), *Building a professional culture in schools* (pp. 45-54). New York: Teachers College Press.

Cronbach, L., & Suppes, P. (1969). *Research for tomorrow's schools: Disciplined inquiry for education.* London: Macmillan.

Cuban, L. (1982). Persistent instruction: The high school classroom 1900-1980. *Phi Delta Kappan, 64*(2), 113-118.

Hatfield, R. C., Blackburn, C. A., & Claypool, C. (1986). *Exploring leadership roles performed by teaching faculty in K-12 schools.* Unpublished paper, Michigan State University for Learning and Teaching, East Lansing.

Johnson, S. M. (1983). Teacher unions in schools: Authority and accommodation. *Harvard Educational Review, 53*(3), 309-326.

Johnson, S. M. (1987). Can schools be reformed at the bargaining table? *Teachers College Record, 89*(2), 269-279.

Kilcher, A. (1990, April). *Leading school reform from the inside and the outside: A case study of teacher leadership.* Paper presented at the American Educational Research Association Annual Meeting, Boston.

Kirchner, D., & Mitchell, P. (1981). *The dynamics of collective bargaining and its impact on governance, administration, and teaching.* Washington, DC: National Institute of Education.

Lieberman, M., & Moskow, M. (1966). *Collective negotiations for teachers: An approach to school administration.* Chicago: Rand McNally.

Little, J. W. (1987). Teachers as colleagues. In V. Richardson-Koehler (Ed.), *Educators handbook: A research perspective* (pp. 491-518). New York: Longman.

Shulman, L. S. (1983). Autonomy and obligation: The remote control of teaching. In L. S. Shulman & G. Sykes (Eds.), *Handbook of teaching and policy* (pp. 484-504). New York: Longman.

Shulman, L. S. (1986). Paradigms and research: A contemporary perspective. In M. Wittrock (Ed.), *The handbook of research on teaching* (3rd ed., pp. 3-36). New York: Macmillan.

Shanker, A. (1986). Teachers must take charge. *Educational Leadership, 44*(1), 12-13.

Sirotnik, K. A., & Clark, R. W. (1988). School-Centered Decision Making. *Phi Delta Kappan, 69*(9), 660-664.

Tambor, J. (1990, April). *Opening classroom doors: Three teachers' journey in creating a new school community*. Paper presented at the American Educational Reform Association Annual Meeting, Boston.

Travers, R. (1983). *How research has changed American schools: A history from 1840 to the present*. Kalamazoo, MI: Mythos Press.

Wasley, Patricia A. (1991). The practical work of teacher leaders: Assumptions, attitudes, and acrophobia. In A. Lieberman & L. Miller (Eds.), *Staff Development for Education in the '90s: New Demands, New Realities, New Perspectives* (pp. 158–183). New York: Teachers College Press.

Index

203

165; and participation, 160; peer relations in a, 3-4, 160; principals in a, 3, 4; and problems of teacher leadership, 160, 162; and professionalism, 16-18; and research about teacher leadership, 24; and roles of teacher leadership, 141; and shared leadership, 164-65; and support/constraints, 141; and Ted Newton, 32, 57, 59-60, 165

Hunter, Madeleine, 66-67, 142, 189. *See also* Instructional Theory Into Practice

Incentives/rewards: and the administration, 159; and collaboration, 153, 160; and Gwen Ingman, 90, 91, 159; as a major issue, 145; and Mary Jones, 102, 103, 105, 109, 128-29, 159, 169, 172; nature of, 159-60; and peer reactions/relations, 159-60; as a problem of teacher leadership, 158-60; and responsibilities, 159; and roles of teacher leaders, 158-60; and school reform, 175, 176; and students, 57, 158-59, 160, 172; for teachers, 159-60; and teaching (profession), 21, 26; and Ted Newton, 55, 57, 158-59, 172; and time, 159

Ingman, Gwen, 66-100 (case study): and assumptions about people/context, 91-92; and definition of teacher leadership, 170-72; dominant themes in, 92-99; and effects of teacher leadership, 157, 169; major issues in, 145-54; and methodology, 187-88, 189-90; overview of, 7; as a person, 69-72, 169, 194; and possibilities for teacher leadership, 169-70; and prescriptive teacher leadership, 90-92, 161-62; and problems of teacher leadership, 169; and rhetoric and reality, 94-95; selection of as a case study, 187-88, 189-90. *See also name of specific topic*

Instruction: assumptions about, 55, 56-57, 161-62, 167-68; attitudes

about, 161-62; and collaboration, 162; and defensive teaching, 16; and definition of teacher leadership, 145, 170-72; evaluation of, 10; and a hierarchical system, 99-100; and problems of teacher leadership, 161-62; and realities of teacher leadership, 156-58; and roles of teacher leadership, 147-49, 154, 161-62, 176, 179-82, 183, 190; teacher-centered, 99-100, 157. *See also* Dailiness of teaching; *name of specific case study*

Instructional Support Teacher (IST) *See* Ingram, Gwen (66-100, passim); Jones, Mary (101-135, passim)

Instructional Theory Into Practice (ITIP). *See* Hunter, Madeleine; Ingman, Gwen (66-100, passim)

Isolation: as characteristic of the teaching profession, 9-10, 21-22; and collaboration, 153; and definition of teacher leadership, 147; and Mary Jones, 108, 126; and methodology, 183, 185-86; and problems of teacher leadership, 160; and realities of teacher leadership, 157; and support/constraints, 137, 141-42

IST. *See* Instructional Support Teacher
ITIP. *See* Instructional Theory Into Practice

Jealousy, 62, 105, 126, 127, 152
Jones, Mary, 101-135 (case study): and assumptions about context/people, 129-30; and definition of teacher leadership, 170-72; dominant themes in, 131-35; and effects of teacher leadership, 157-58, 169; major issues in, 145-54; metaphors in, 131-32; and methodology, 187-90; overview of, 7; as a person, 106-10, 127, 194; and possibilities for teacher leadership, 169-70; and realities of teacher leadership, 157-58; selection of as a case study, 187-89. *See also name of specific topic*

About the Author

Patricia A. Wasley is the Senior Researcher for Change at the Coalition of Essential Schools at Brown University, and currently represents the Coalition in a variety of national symposia on school restructuring throughout the United States. She completed her Ed.D. at the University of Washington, and was the Project Director of the Teacher Leadership Strand of the Puget Sound Educational Consortium (PSEC), in Seattle. Before becoming a specialist in curricular and pedagogical change, Pat Wasley spent a year learning from fourth graders. Prior to that she was a high school English teacher and an administrator in a regional educational agency. She is currently writing her second book about how teachers change classroom practices on behalf of student learning.